Beginning
Map Skills

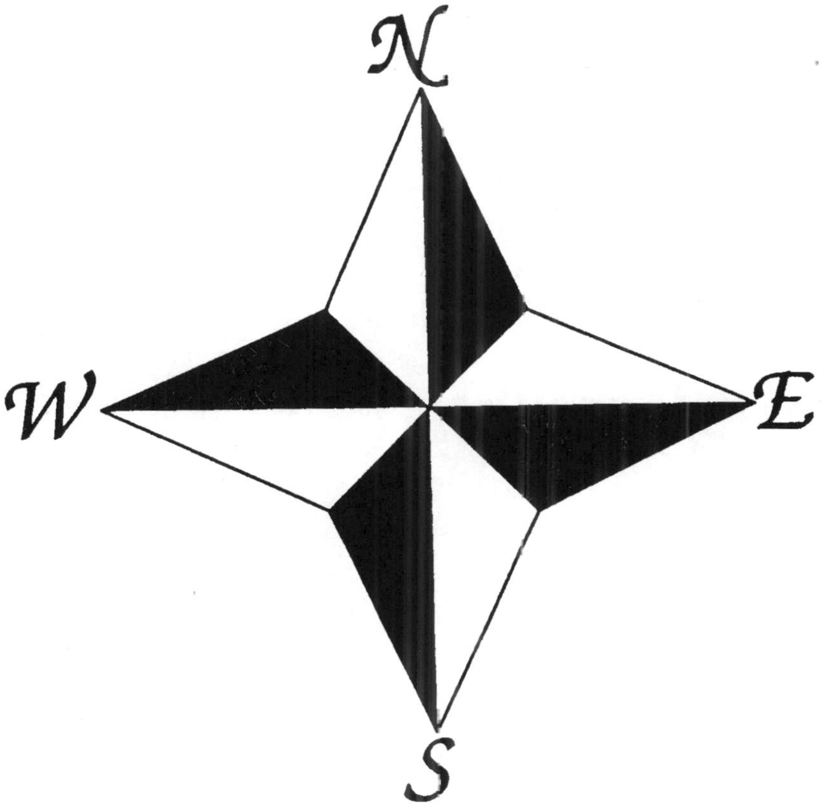

Written by John and Patty Carratello

Illustrated by Paula Spence and Keith Vasconcelles

Teacher Created Resources
6421 Industry Way
Westminster, CA 92683
www.teachercreated.com
ISBN: 978-1-55734-167-9
©1990 Teacher Created Resources
Reprinted, 2014
Made in U.S.A.

Table of Contents

Introduction

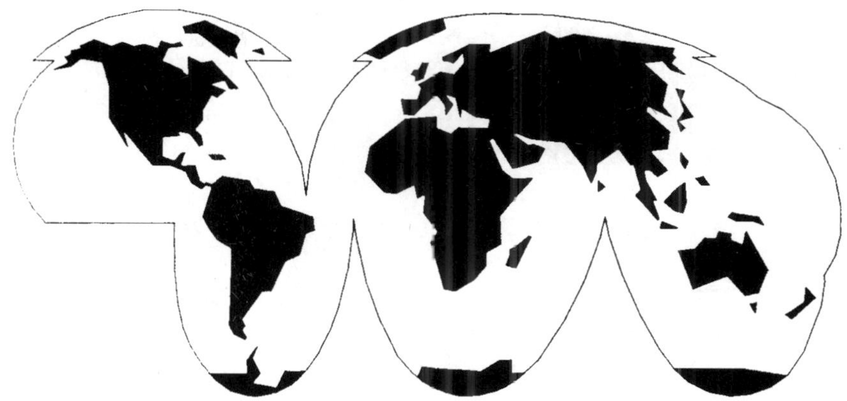

Beginning MAP SKILLS

One of a child's earliest opportunities to communicate with others is through pictures. He learns the ideas of others when he looks at pictures and talks about what he sees. She lets others know what she is thinking when she draws a picture and tells an interested person about what she has drawn.

*A **map** is a picture. It is a visual way to communicate information about all kinds of things, from the floor plans of a child's bedroom to a mysterious, fictional treasure map. From a map, a child can gather and share an abundance of information about the real or imagined world in which he or she lives.*

Beginning MAP SKILLS *contains activities geared to primary children who are learning basic map skills. The progression of skills taught is gradual, and skills once learned are reinforced in subsequent activities. Successful completion of these activities will produce eager mapmakers, on their way to becoming more visually literate readers.*

What Is a Map?

A *map* is a picture that shows us a place. The place a map shows us can be anywhere! A map can be drawn of our room, our street, our school, our city, our country, our world, or our solar system. A map can show us what it looks like in our bodies, under a city, or beneath the ocean. We can even make a map of a pretend world!

What places do these maps show us? Use the places in the word box to help you.

room	**city**	**world**
school	**country**	**solar system**
street	**body**	**pretend world**

1. ______________________________

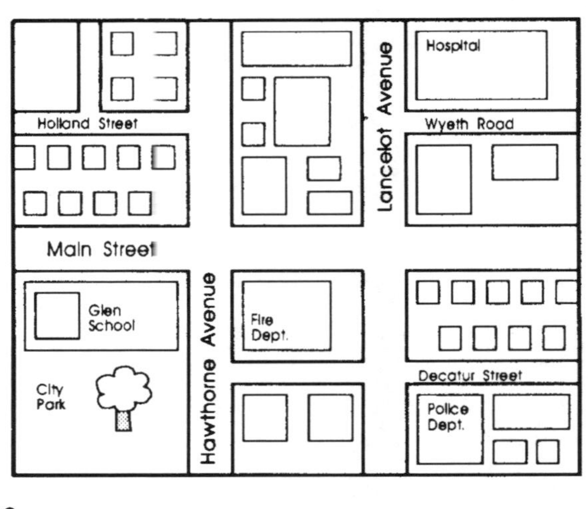

2. ______________________________

3. ______________________________

4. ______________________________

Early Maps

Suppose you live in a time long, long ago. You decide to go to a special spot to play and want your friend to come with you. But your friend is not awake and you don't want to wait. Your friend's mother suggests you leave your friend a note outside the entrance to the cave.

You can not write and your friend can not read, but you can draw and your friend can understand pictures. The spot where you want to play is next to the tall oak tree by the pond. You will be sitting on the large flat rock by the tree. Draw this message for your friend in the dirt outside his or her cave.

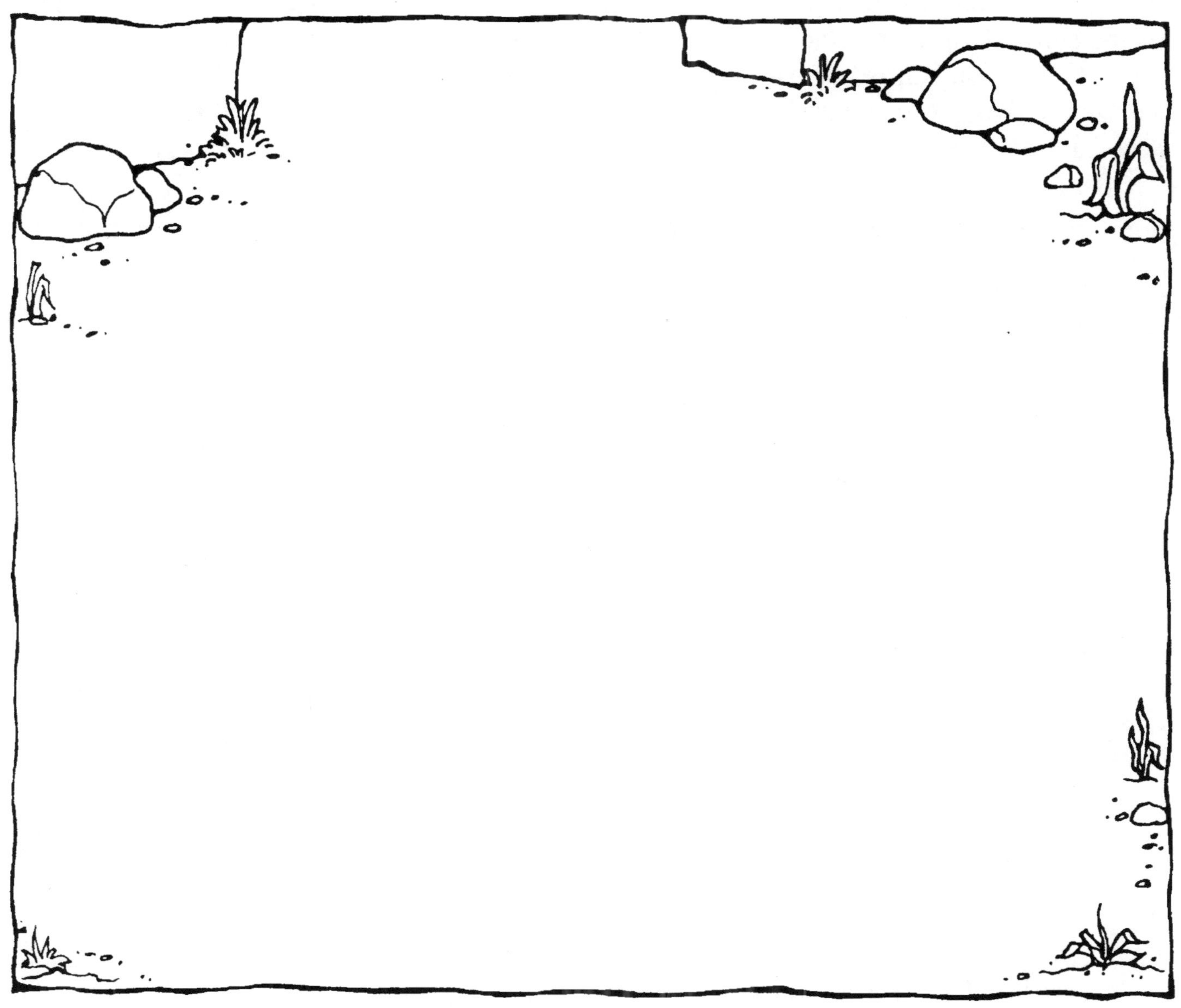

Early maps were made like this. Sometimes they were drawn in dirt or carved in tree bark. Sometimes they were marked in clay or chiseled in stone. All these early maps told people who drew or read them something about their world.

Early Maps Get Better

Early maps, like those made in dirt, bark, clay, or stone, helped people know more about where they were or wanted to be.

As time went on, mapmakers wanted to make better maps. They began to use the position of the sun to help them place things on their maps. For example, one town may be more toward the sun at sunrise than another. The lake was always on the right side of the sunrise. The forest was on the sunset side of the canyon. Early mapmakers began to place things according to direction. We know these directions as *north, south, east,* and *west.*

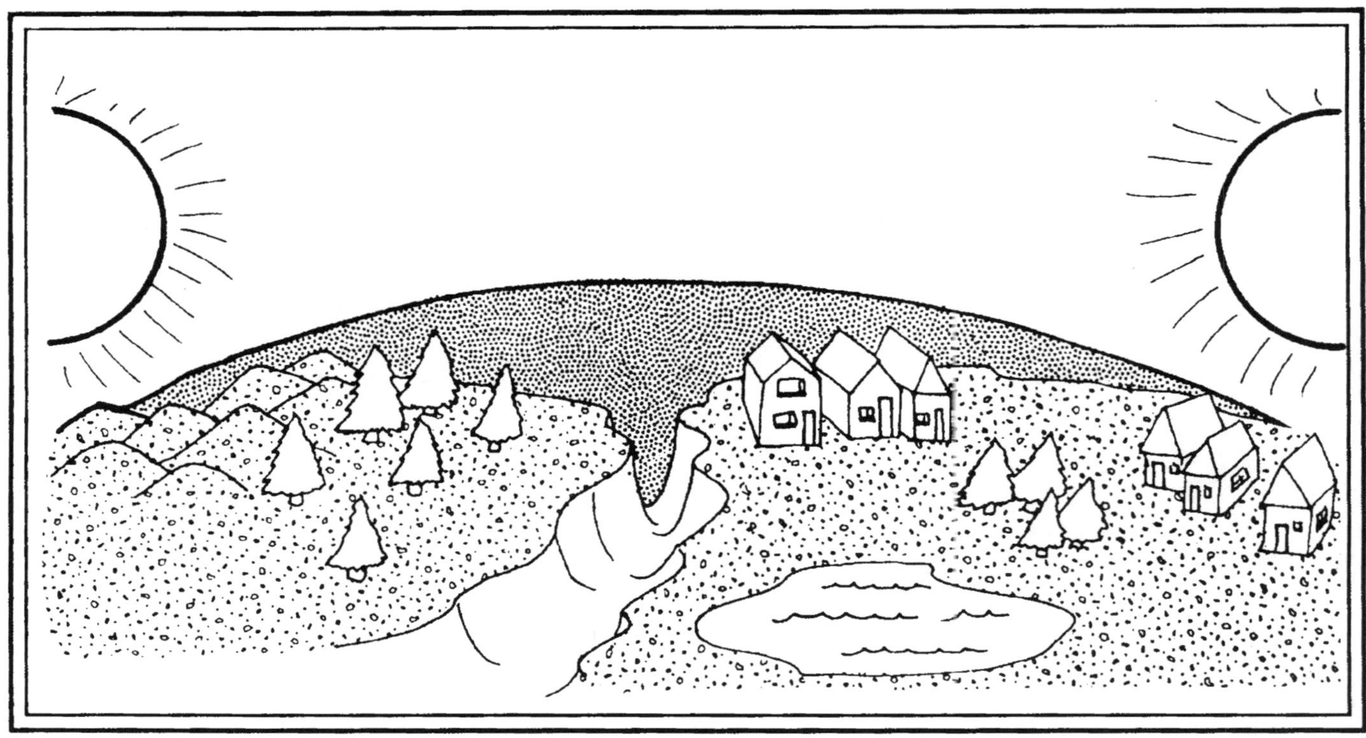

As maps became better, people began to use them more. They wanted maps that could be more easily carried than the maps made on clay or treebark. Maps were made on animal skins and on cloth. You might be interested to know that the word map comes from the Latin word *mappa. Mappa* means napkin or cloth. Later, after paper was invented, maps were made on paper.

Can you think of some things to draw maps on?

The Parts of a Map

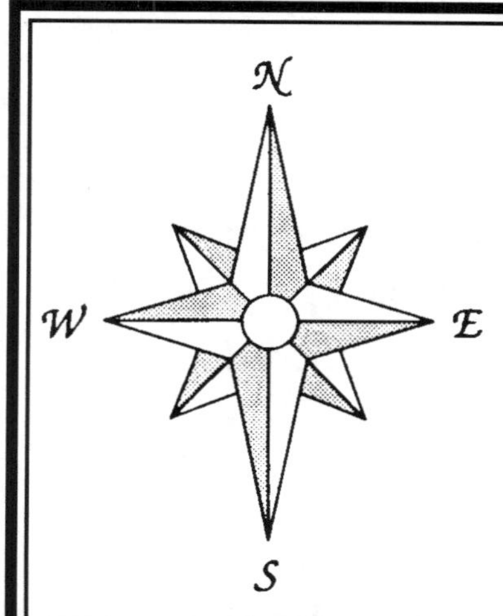

Most maps have parts that are the same. You will learn about these parts in this book.

Maps have some way of showing the directions north, south, east, and west.

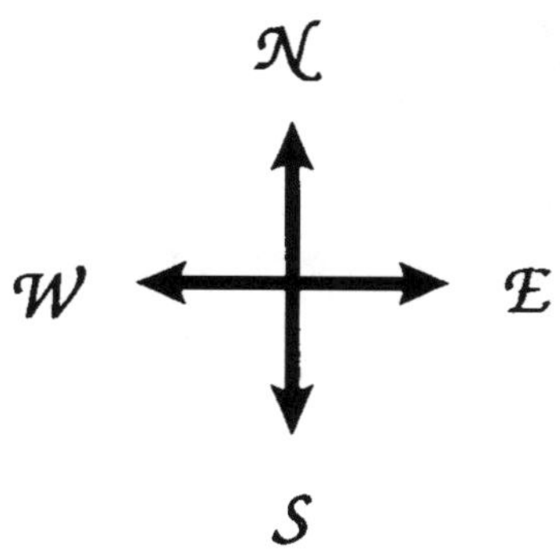

*Maps have **symbols** that standfor things that are drawn on a map. These symbols are explained on a map key.*

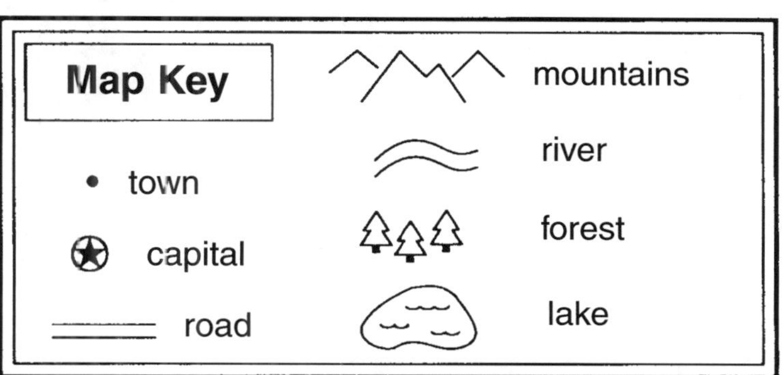

Scale

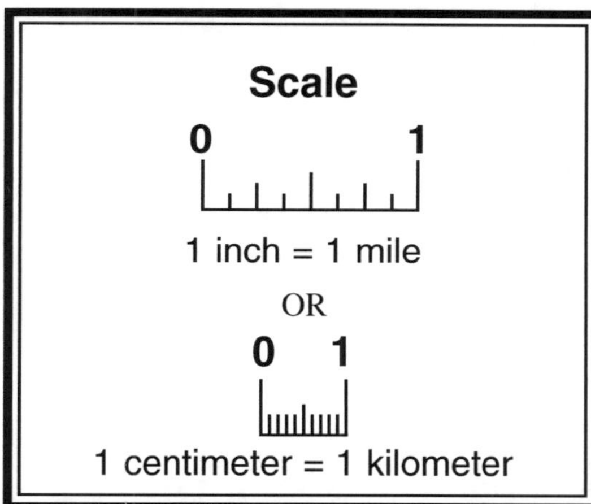

*Maps have **scales** to show us a way to measure distance. Mapmakers usually have to draw things smaller on their maps than they really are.*

*Maps have **titles**. The title tells us what the map is about.*

*Maps have **labels**. Labels tell us what things on the map are.*

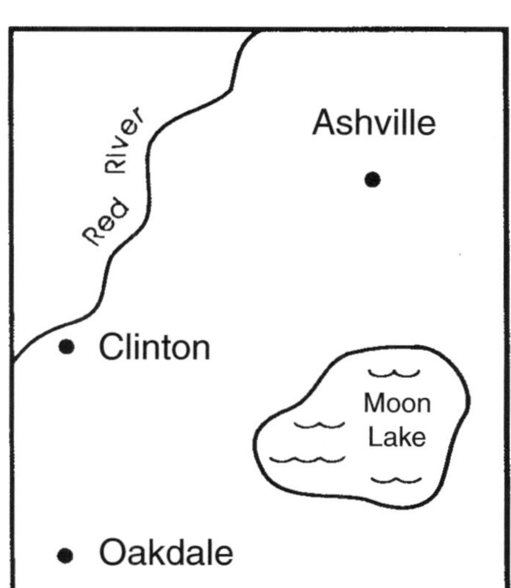

Can you name the parts of a map?

Do You Know Your Directions?

There are four main directions to know as we learn our way around the world in which we live. These directions are *north, south, east,* and *west.* If we know these directions, it will be easier for us to tell where we are and where we would like to go.

Here are what the directions look like on a piece of paper.

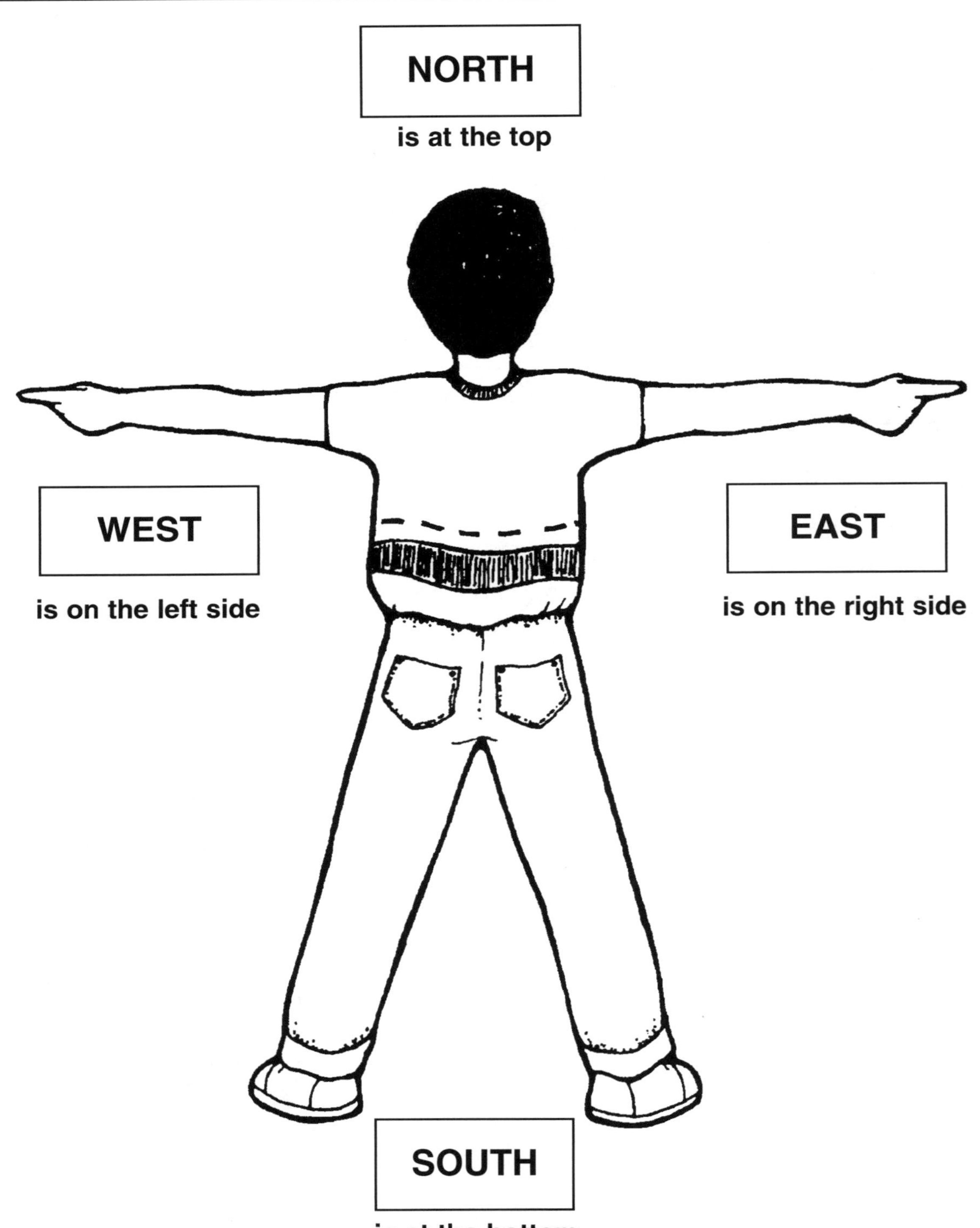

North, South, East, or West?

Fill in the direction words that are missing.

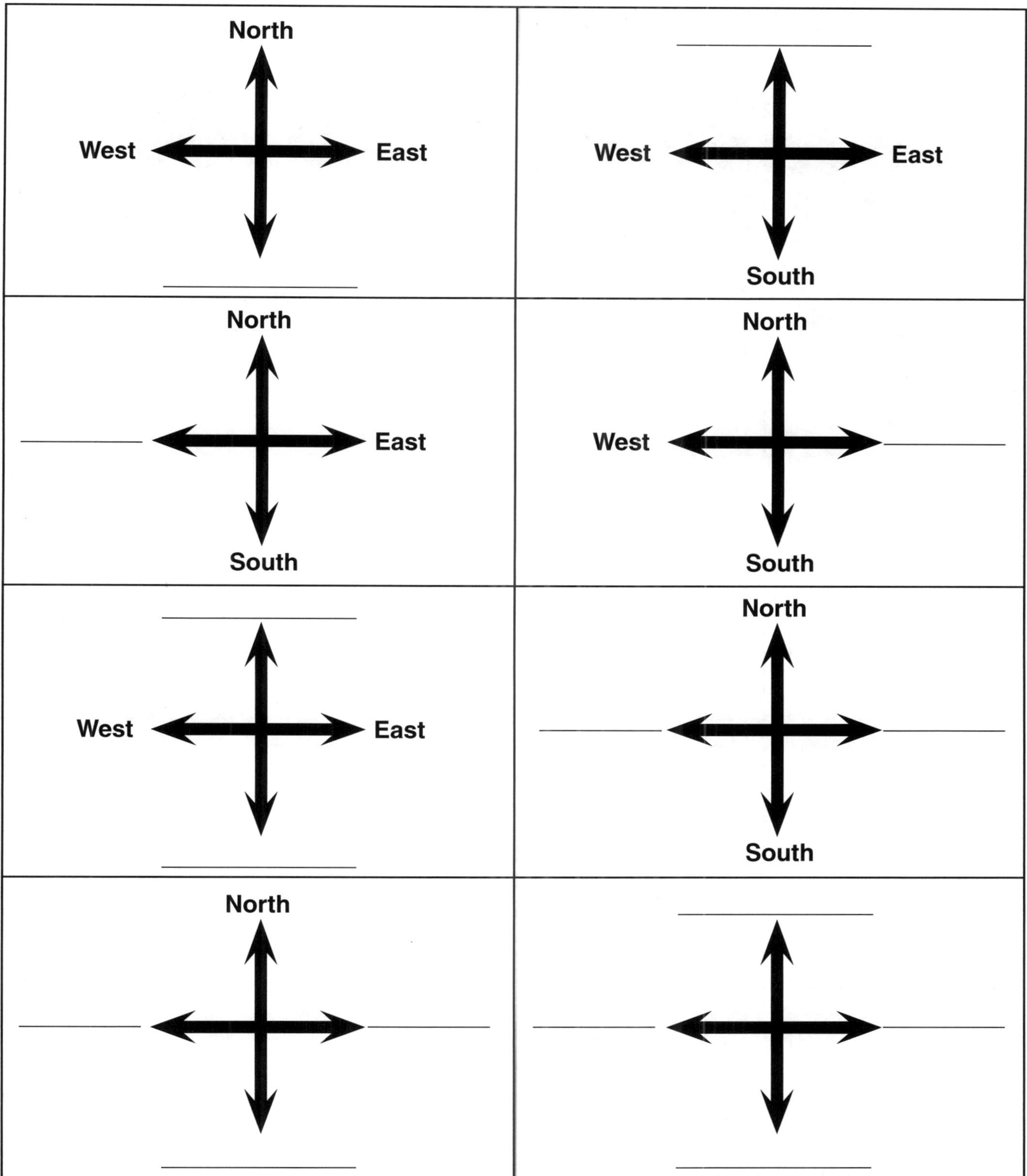

Through the Squares

Can you find your way through the squares by following the directions? Color your path as you go.

1. Start **above** the square marked **start here.**

2. Go **south** 5 squares.

3. Go **east** 2 squares.

4. Go **north** 3 squares.

5. Go **east** 4 squares.

6. Go **south** 2 squares.

7. Go **west** 3 squares.

8 Go **south** 3 squares.

9 Go **west** 4 squares.

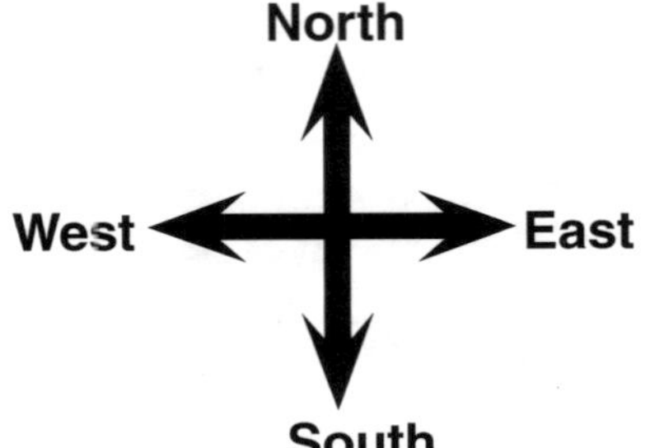

Start here

Color the square where you finish your favorite color!

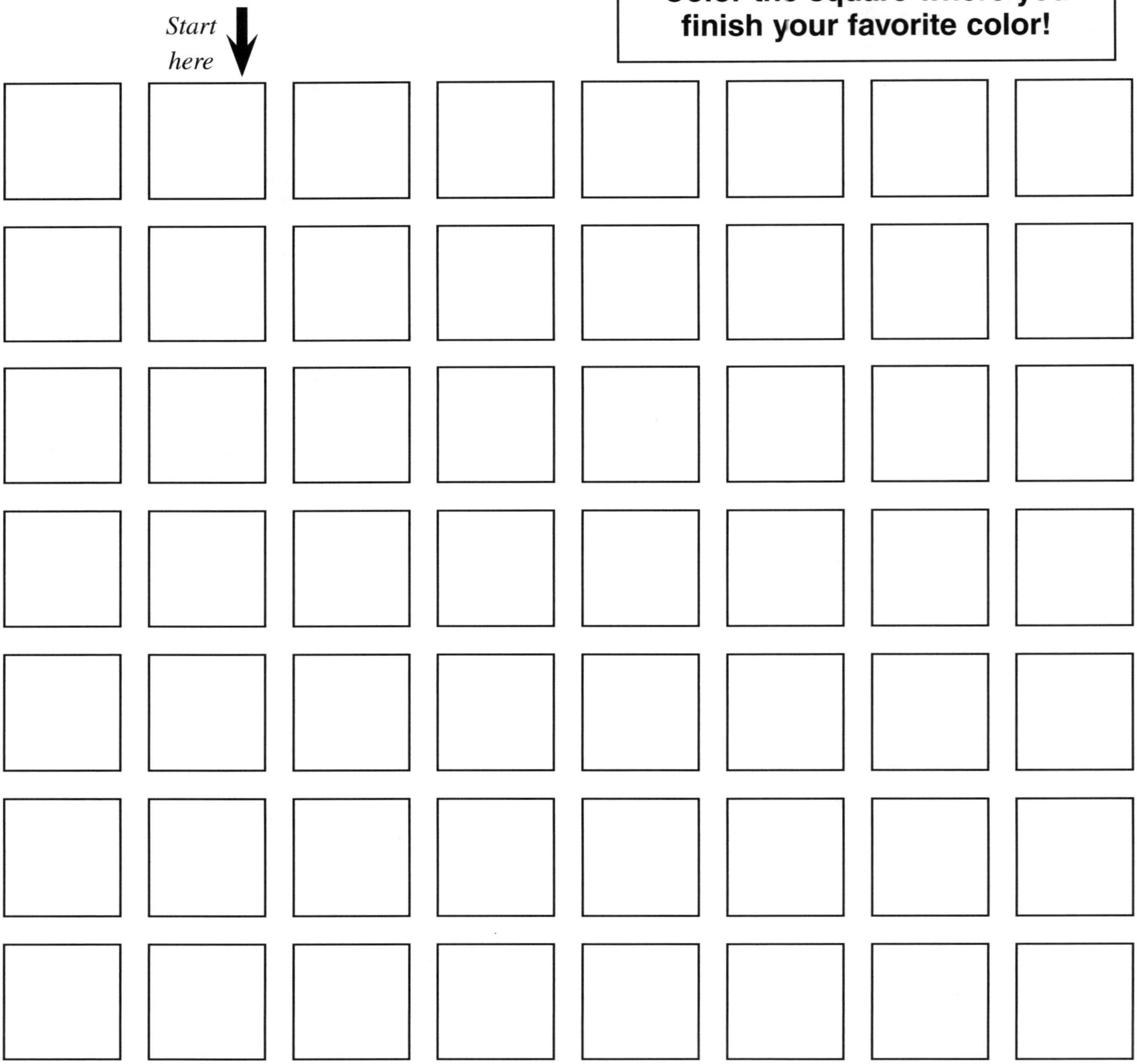

Directions Quiz!

1. What are the four main directions?

   ______________   ________________   ________________   ________________

2. What directions are opposite from each other?

   __________________ is the opposite of __________________

   __________________ is the opposite of __________________

3. If a map is drawn on a piece of paper, what direction is:

   at the top of the page? __________________

   at the bottom of the page? __________________

   on the left side of the page? __________________

   on the right side of the page? __________________

4. In the box to the right, label the arrows with the directions that show a picture of what you wrote to answer question #3.

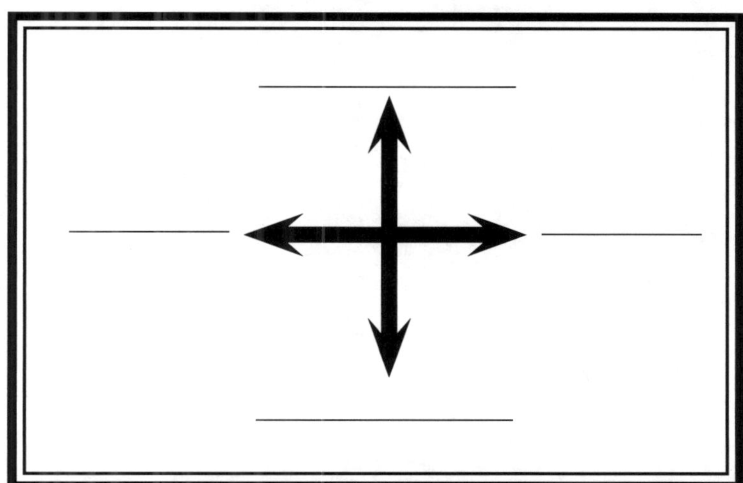

5. What two directions are next to west?

   ___**north**___   ________________

6. What two directions are next to east?

   ________________   ________________

7. What two directions are next to south?

   ________________   ___**east**___

8. What two directions are next to north?

   ________________   ________________

Which Way Should We Go?

Can you help the child find the playground? Tell him how many steps he should take north, south, east, and west.

The first footprint is the first step.

Take **3** steps **south** .	Take ___ steps _______ .
Take ___ steps _______ .	Take ___ steps _______ .
Take ___ steps _______ .	Take ___ steps _______ .
Take ___ steps _______ .	Take ___ steps _______ .
Take ___ step _______ .	Take ___ steps _______ .

Direct Me, Sun!

You can find your directions with the help of the sun! Here's how!

At noon*, turn toward the sun. You will be facing **south**. Do not look directly at the sun.

Think about it:

Do you think you could find your directions at sunrise and sunset? (Do you know the sun rises in the east and sets in the west?)

If you are using daylight savings time, face the sun at 1:00 p.m.

Thanks, Sun!

The sun rises in the east.

The sun sets in the west.

1. ________________________

2. ________________________

3. When you face the sunrise (**east**), **north** is on your left, **south** is on your right, and _______ is behind you.

4. When you face the sunset (**west**), **north** is on your right, **south** is on your left, and _______ is behind you.

Direct Me, Stars!

You have learned that you can find your directions with the help of the sun at sunrise, noon, and sunset. You also can find your directions with the help of the stars if it is a clear night!

Here's how.

Locate the constellation, or group of stars, called the Big Dipper. It is made up of seven stars and looks like this.

It looks like a big dipper for water in the sky!

Can you find it?

- Look at the Big Dipper again.

- Find the "pointer stars" at the side of the dipper that is farthest away from the handle.

- Make a straight line up from the pointer stars. They point to the North Star.

- Face the North Star and you are facing **north**. Behind you is **south**. To your right is **east**, and to your left is **west**.

The North Star is a very bright star that always seems to stay in the same position.

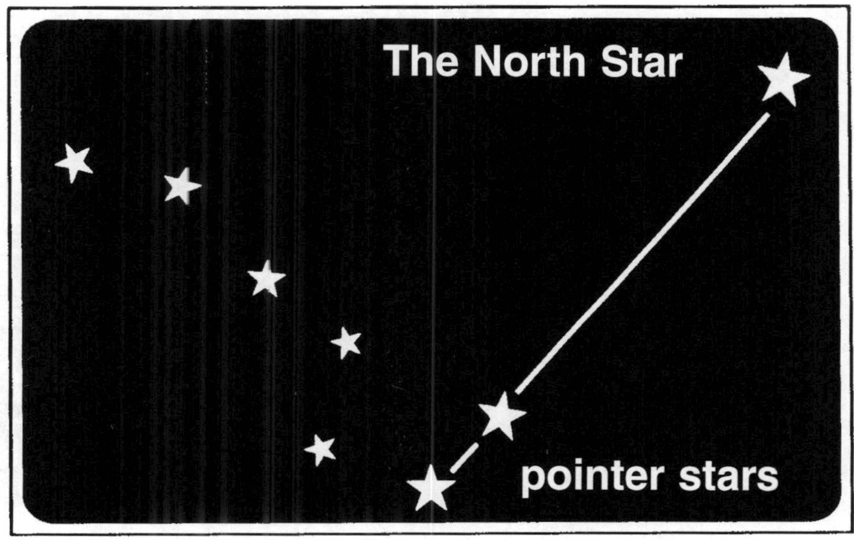

Find the North Star!

Look at the sky on this starry night. Trace the outline of the Big Dipper. Circle the North Star.

The Big Dipper is part of the constellation Ursa Major (Big Bear). Polaris is another name for the North Star.

More Directions!

You have learned four directions, *north, south, east,* and *west*. But sometimes people need more direction to find where they want to go. They don't always travel straight north or south, east or west! Here are some more words to help people find their way.

northeast

    is halfway between north and east

northwest

    is halfway between north and west

southeast

    is halfway between south and east

southwest

    is halfway between south and west

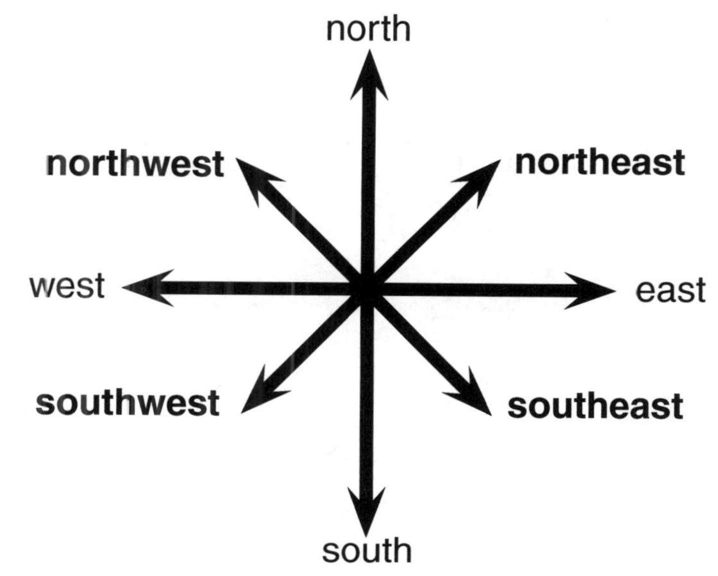

As you can see, the new direction words are made by combining the direction words you have already learned. The words have to be combined in a certain way. The words north and south always come first.

Cross out the direction words that are not combined correctly.

southwest	**westnorth**
northwest	**eastsouth**
westsouth	**northeast**
eastnorth	**southeast**

The Compass Rose

This is a *compass rose*. A *compass rose* is a symbol mapmakers use to show direction.

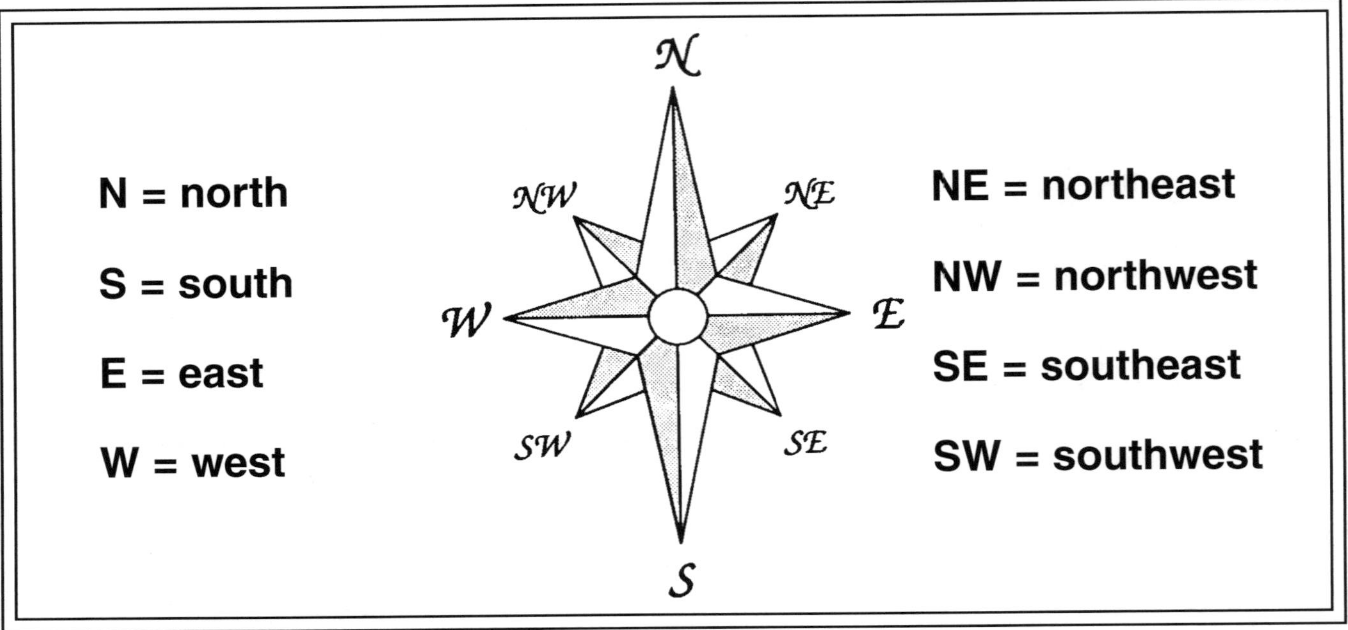

N = north   NE = northeast

S = south   NW = northwest

E = east   SE = southeast

W = west   SW = southwest

*Answer these questions about the **compass rose.***

1. Which direction points to the top of the page?

____

2. Which points of the compass rose are the longest?

_______________ and _______________

3. What direction is between south and west?

____

4. How many directions are shown on this compass rose?

____

5. What direction is opposite of northwest?

____

6. What direction is opposite of southwest?

____

7. What two directions are next to east?

_______________ and _______________

Your Compass Rose

Use the pieces on pages 19 and 20 to make your own compass rose.

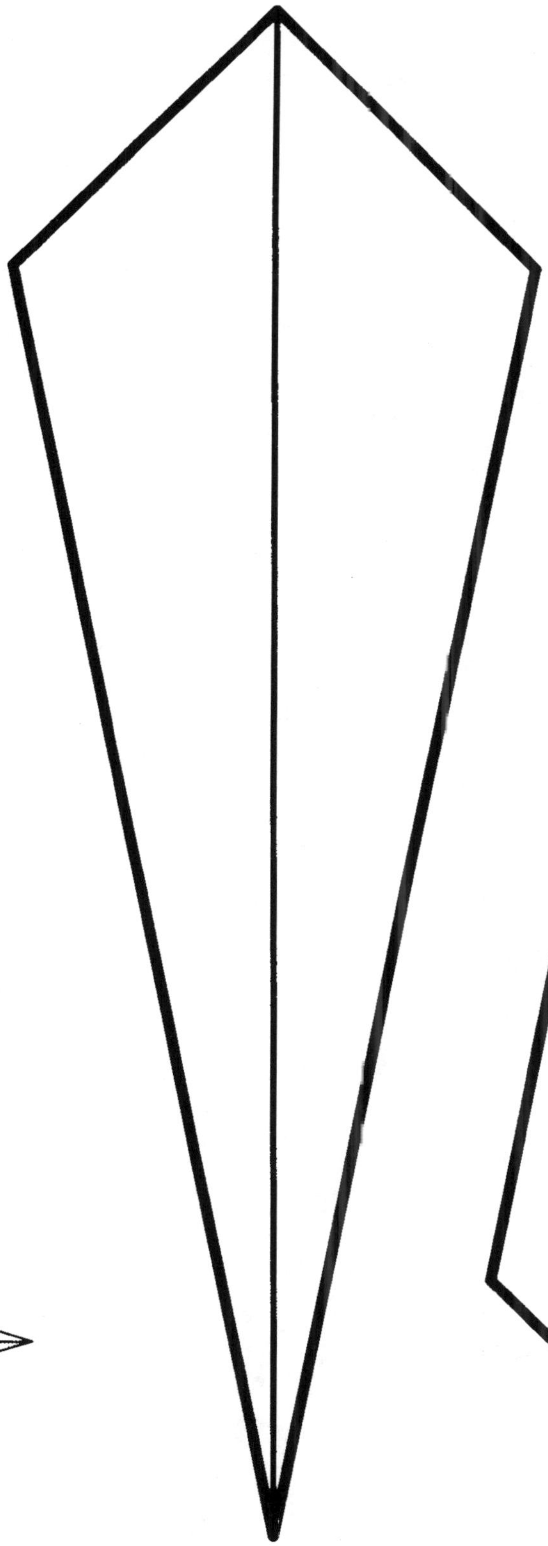

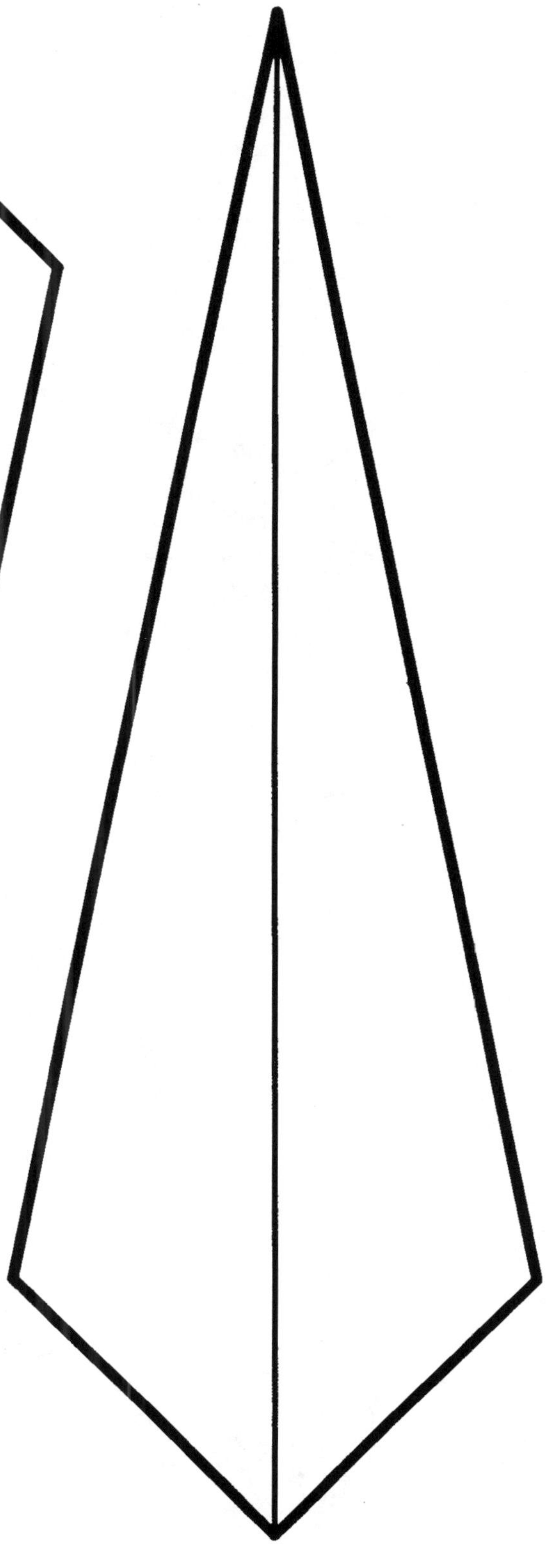

1. Cut out all the pieces on pages 19 and 20.

2. Arrange them correctly on a large piece of paper. *

3. Attach the pieces in their correct spots with glue or paste.

4. Label the directional points on the paper.

5. Color your compass rose.

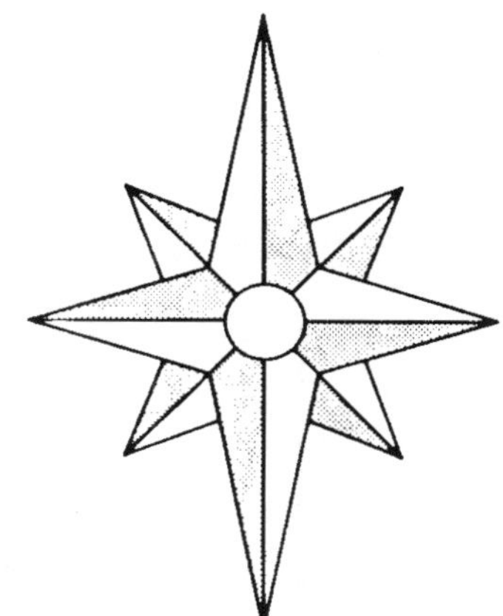

* The north and south points are longer than the other directional points.

Your Compass Rose *(cont.)*

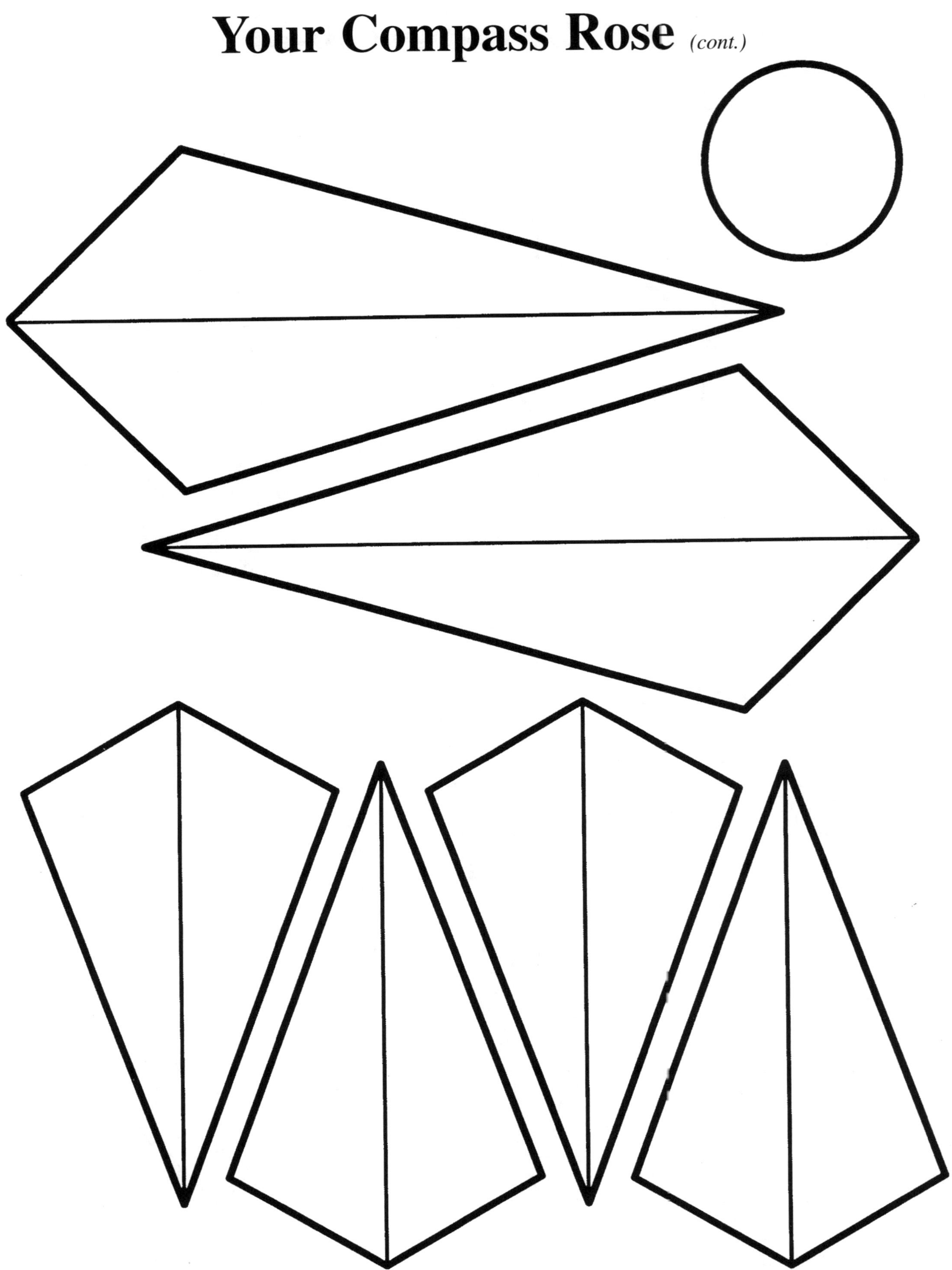

What Is Where?

Can you use your compass rose to explain in which direction things are in your room?

Step 1   Find where **north** is in your room. Use the position of the sun at sunrise or sunset to help you.

Step 2   While you are in your room, make your compass rose point **north**.

Step 3   Write down the name of something in your room that is in **each** of these eight directions.

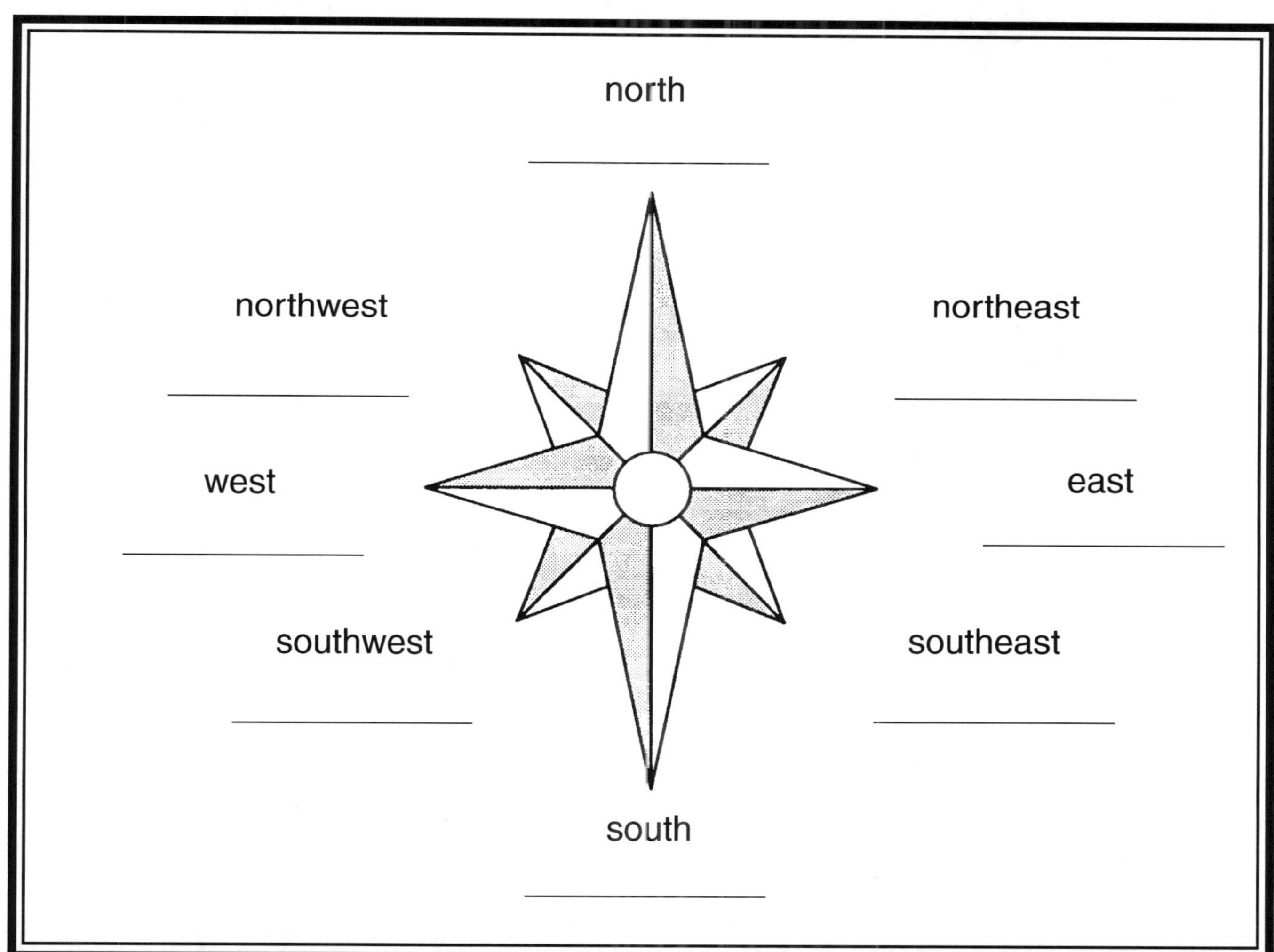

Try this in other places, too! Can you find the direction of things in the park? Can you describe the direction people sit in the classroom? Do you know in which direction things are from your house? Try it!

Magnetic North

You have learned to find your directions by the position of the sun and the stars. You can also find your way with the help of a *compass*!

Compass

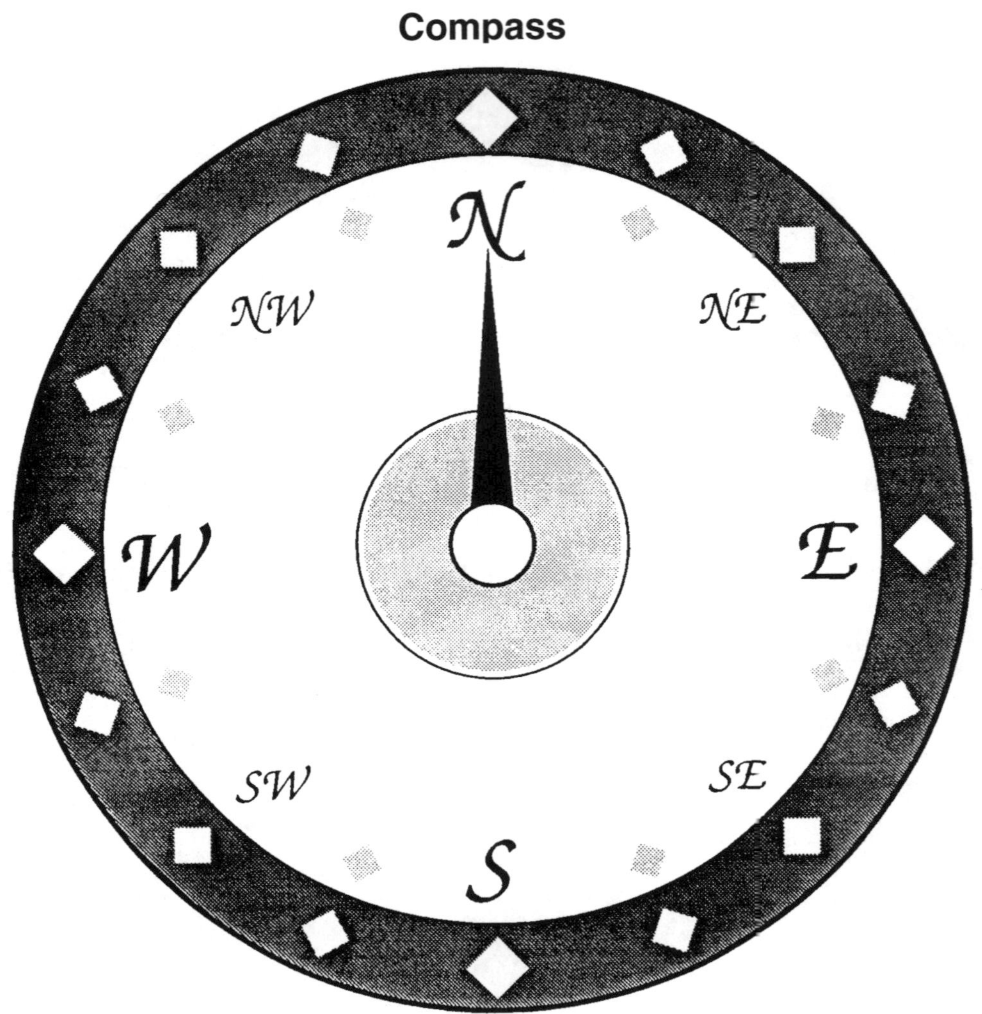

A *compass* is an instrument that has a moveable needle in it that always points to "magnetic" north. The magnetic pull of the needle is caused when the north magnetic pole and the south magnetic pole of the Earth line up. These poles attract the compass needle, which will always point to magnetic north. Magnetic north is **sometimes** a little different from the north that is shown by the position of the sun and the stars. But the needle always points in a northerly direction.

Where Am I?

You have lost your way in the woods. You have a canteen and a compass with you and you know you must try to get back to your campsite before dark. Your camp is northeast of the waterfall and you remember that you must travel south and east to get around some large rock formations before you reach the trail north to your camp. Your compass tells you that you are now facing north.

Trace the path your compass shows you to take.

Symbols

A *symbol* is something that stands for something else. For example, a "+" stands for add and a "-" stands for subtract. A heart is a symbol for love and a flag is the symbol for a country. There are many other symbols we use, too.

Use the words in the box to help you label these symbols.

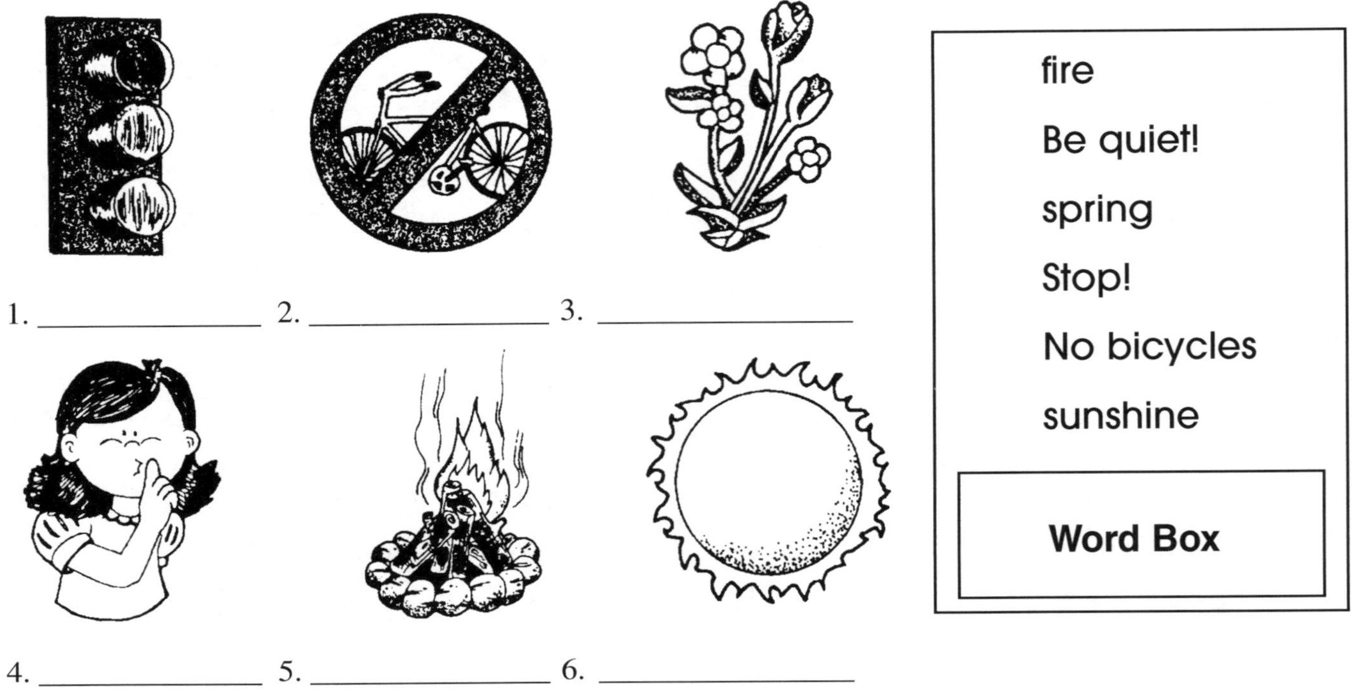

1. _______________   2. _______________   3. _______________

4. _______________   5. _______________   6. _______________

> **Maps also use symbols. Symbols** *on a map stand for things that are in the place the map shows us.*

What kinds of *symbols* do you think might be used to show us these things on maps? Draw your ideas in the boxes.

a playground	a house	a lake	mountains

Symbols on Maps

A Key

Look at this map and the map *key*. Use it to answer the questions below.

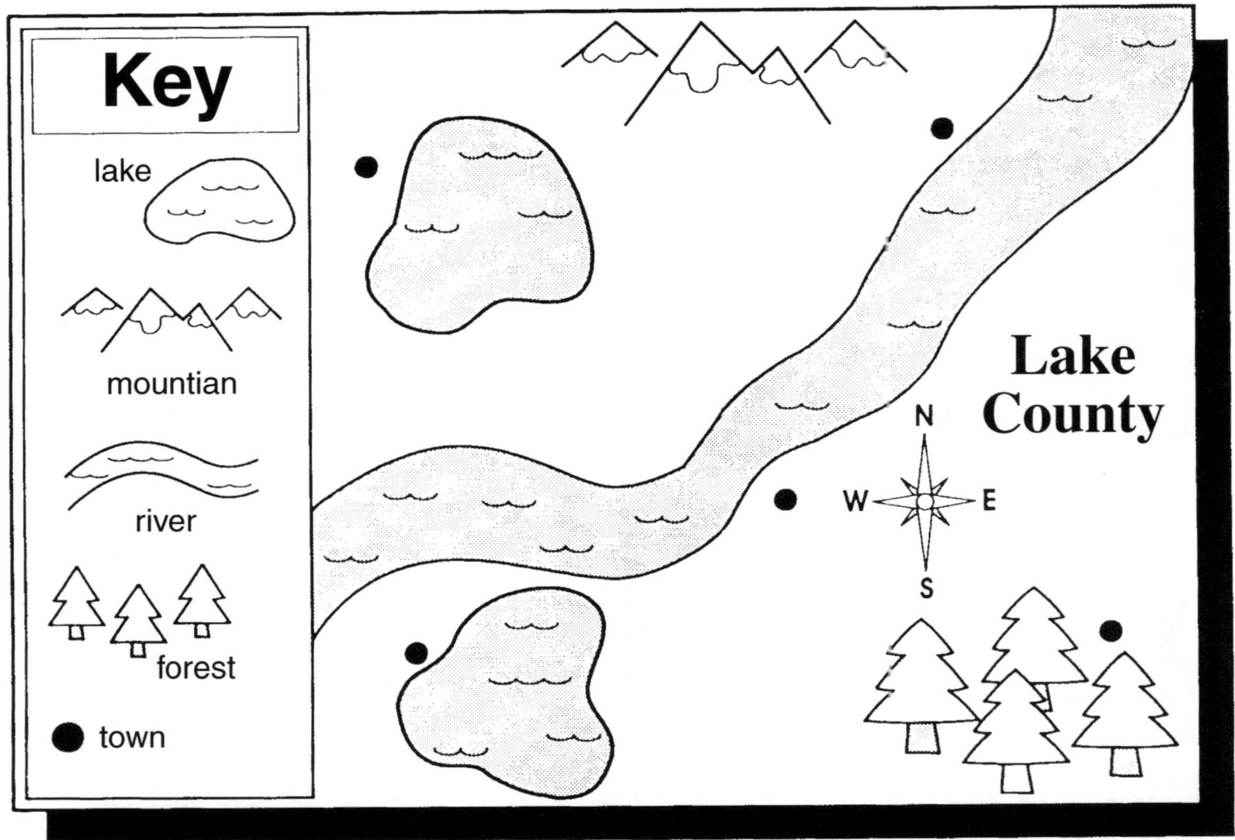

1. There are ________________________ lakes in Lake County.

2. There are ________________________ towns in Lake County.

3. One of the towns in Lake County is not by water. It is by the

   f________________________ .

4. Between a lake and the river, there are **m**________________________ at the

   north end of Lake County.

5. A **r**________________ runs through the middle of the county between two lakes.

You Make the Key!

Read the map on this page. Then draw the correct symbols next to each word in the key.

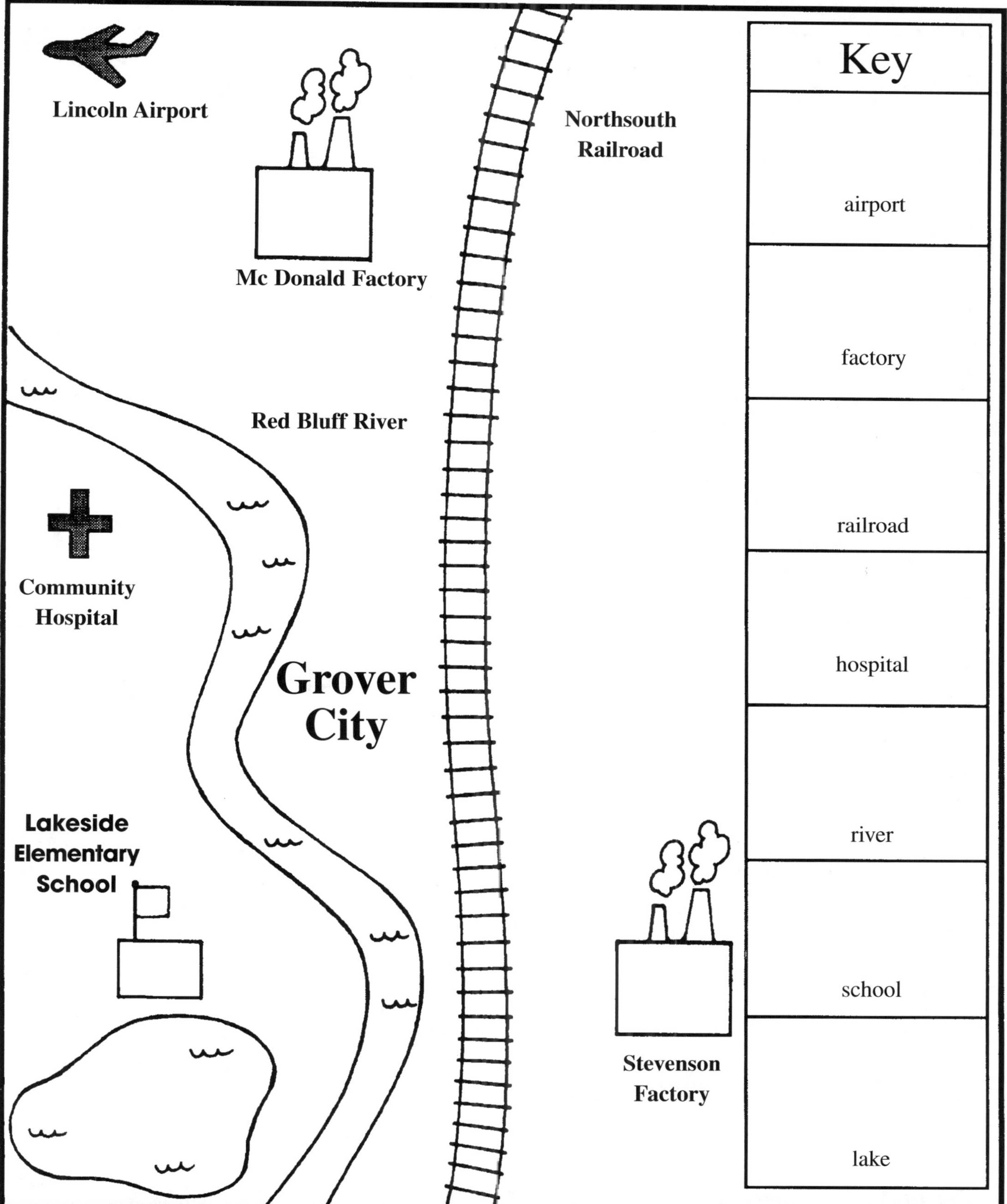

Neighborhood Map

Look carefully at this map. Then answer the questions at the bottom of the page.

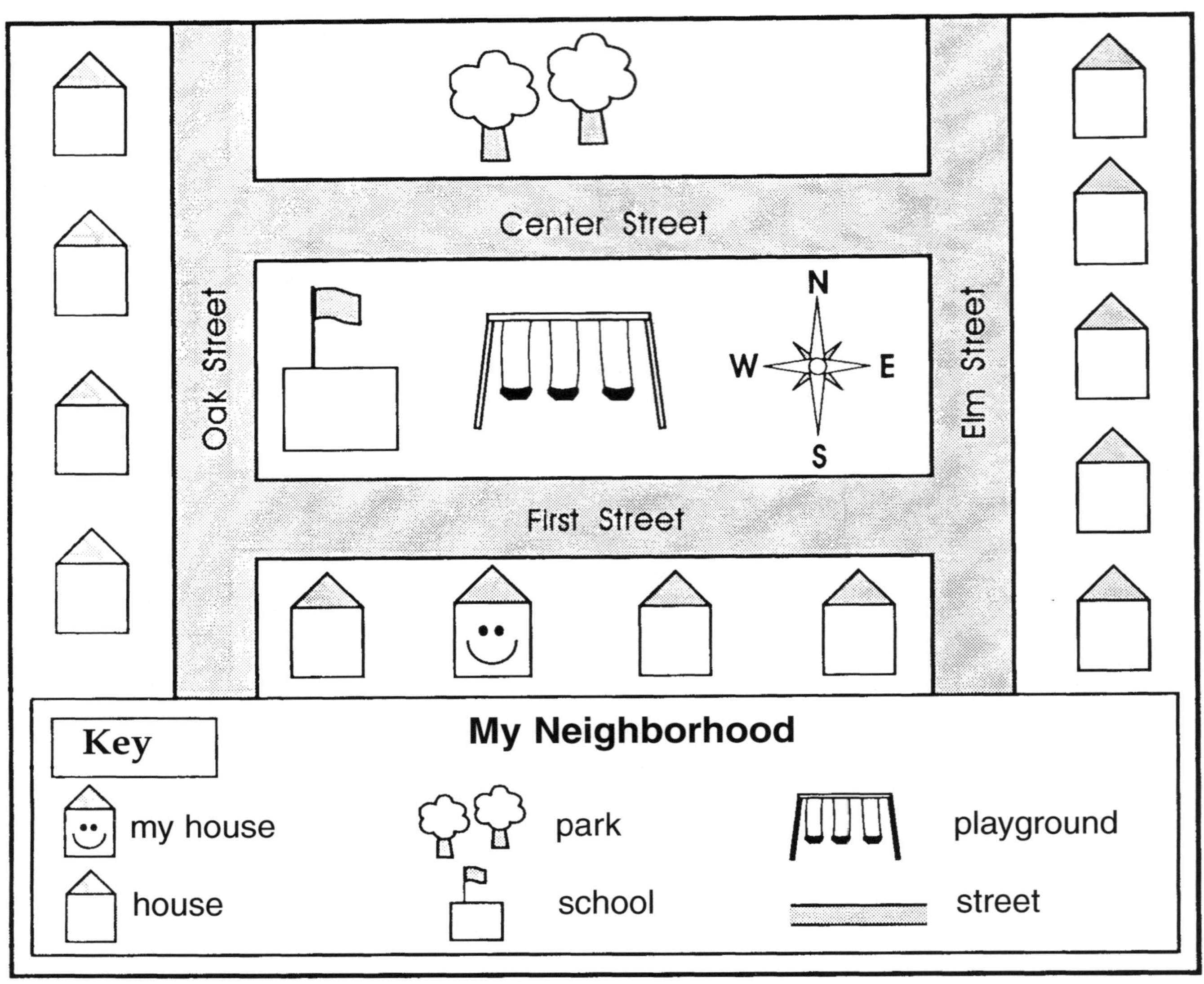

1. The ___________________ is west of the playground.

2. My house is ___________________ of First Street. (north, east, west, or south)

3. To get from the school to the park, you must cross ___________________ Street.

4. There are ___________________ houses east of Elm Street.

5. The school is on the land between ___________________ Street,

___________________ Street, ___________________ Street,

and ___________________ Street.

My Perfect Place

Draw a map of the perfect place for you to live. Use your imagination! You may live by a lake, your school playground, an amusement park, or your best friend. Make a key for the symbols you use.

Mapmaking

When mapmakers draw maps, they usually have to make the things and places on the maps fit together like they do in the real world. A lake needs to take up the same amount of space on a map as it does in the real world. A bed should cover the same area on a room map as it does in a bedroom. Oceans need to cover as much space on a globe as they do on Earth.

Can you imagine how big a map of the world would have to be if it had to be drawn the same size as the **real** world? How about your city? What about your school or your classroom? Could you draw a map of your bedroom on paper the same size as your room?

Think of two things that could be drawn on a map the same size as they are.

1. _______________________ 2. _______________________

Think of two things that could never be drawn on a map the same size they are.

1. _______________________ 2. _______________________

Scale

Mapmakers can make things on a map larger or smaller than they really are. We can do this by using a map *scale*. This map scale shows us a way to measure distance. We are told by the scale what kind of measurement equals what kind of distance.

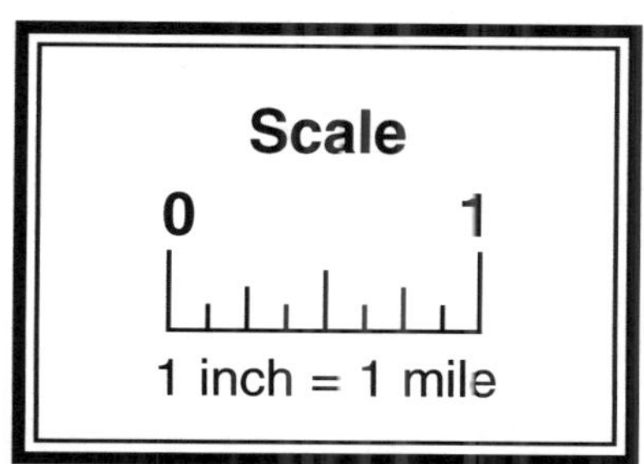

Look at this scale. 1 inch stands for 1 mile. If something was 2 miles long it would be shown as 2 inches. If it was 5 miles long, it would be shown as 5 inches.

Use the scale on this page to answer these questions about the map below.

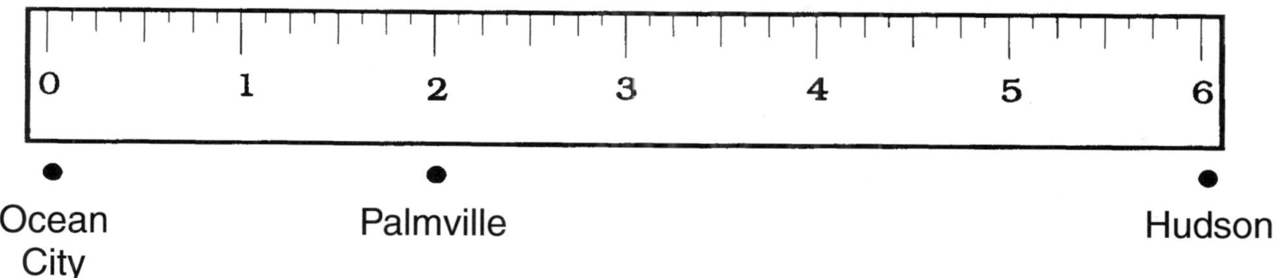

1. 1 inch equals how many miles? ____

2. How many inches is it from Ocean City to Palmville? _______________________

   How many miles? ____

3. How many inches is it from Ocean City to Hudson? _______________________

   How many miles? ____

4. How many miles is it from Palmville to Ocean City? _______________________

5. How many inches is it from Palmville to Hudson? _______________________

   How many miles? ____

How Many Miles?

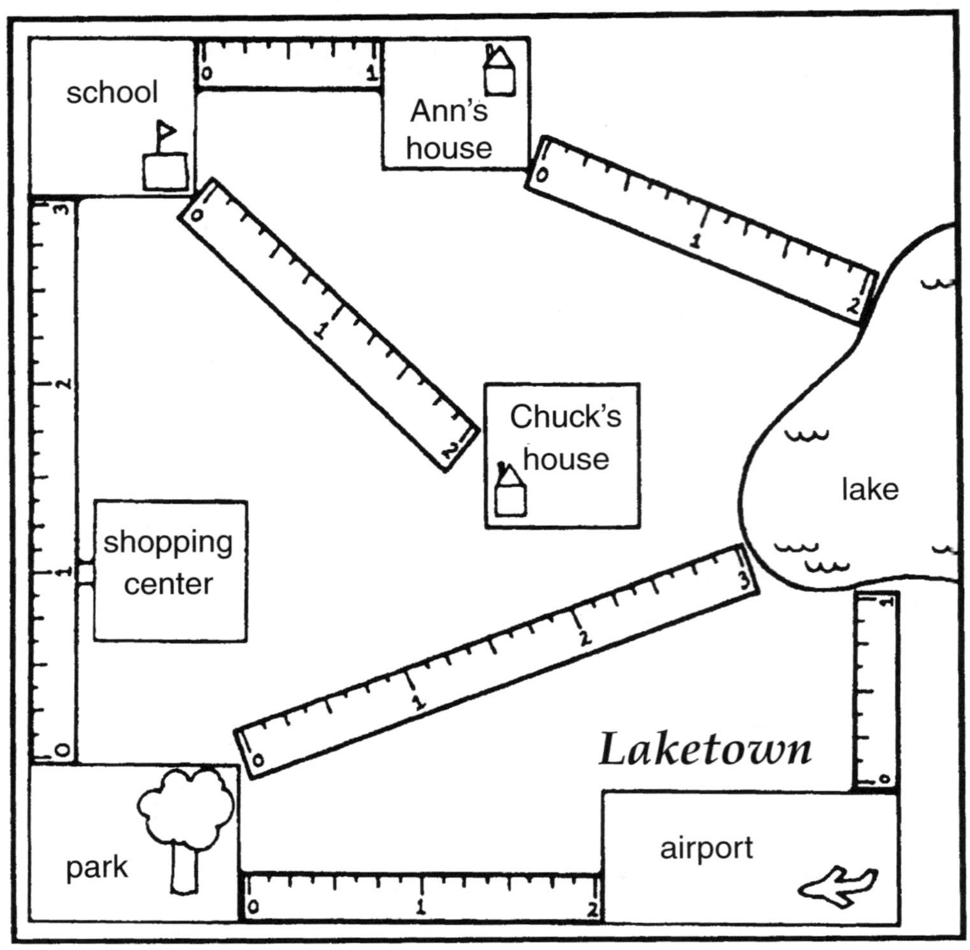

Look at the map of an imaginary city called Laketown. Can you use the map scale and the map to answer questions about distance?

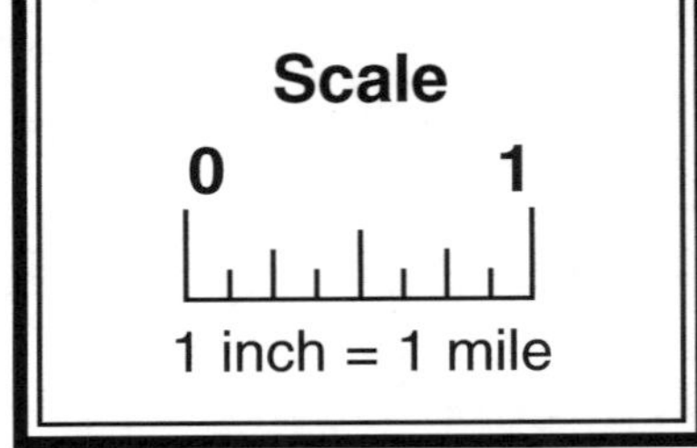

1. There is one inch between Ann's house and the school.

   How far is her house from school? _______________________________

2. There are two inches between the park and the airport. _______________________

   How many miles are they from each other? _______________________

3. How many inches are between the park and the school? _______________________

   How many miles are they apart? _______________________

4. How many miles is the lake from the park? _______________________

5. How far is the school from the shopping center? _______________________

6. How far is the lake from Ann's house? _______________________

7. How far is the school from Chuck's house? _______________________

8. What is the distance between the lake and the airport in miles? _______________________

9. How far is the park from the shopping center? _______________________

Choosing Your Scale

We use a map scale to show a way to measure distance. When we choose a scale to use, it needs to be suited to the type of map we are making.

- If we use the scale of 1 inch = 1 mile to draw a map of a bedroom, we would not be able to see the map! Our bedrooms can't be measured in miles!

- If we used the scale of 1 inch = 1 mile to draw a map of our solar system, we would not have enough paper for our map!

We need to choose a scale that "fits" what we map.

Match the map with the scale that is best for it.

1. A map of your bedroom

   Scale # _______________________________

2. A map of a city and the area around it

   Scale # _______________________________

3. A map of our solar system

   Scale # _______________________________

4. A map of a birdhouse

   Scale # _______________________________

5. A map of North America

   Scale # _______________________________

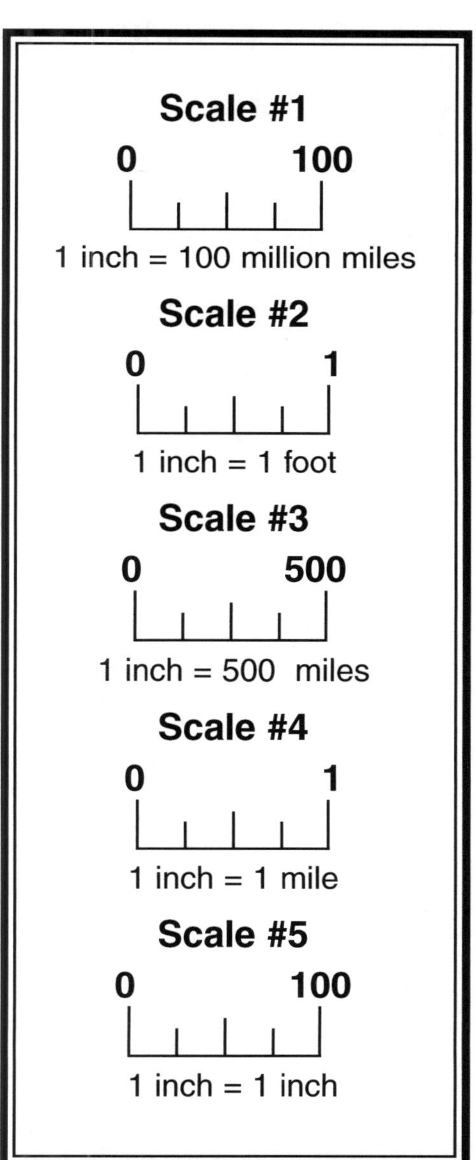

Measurement

Measurement for a map scale can be given in *inches*, *feet*, or *miles*. This type of measurement is called *standard measure*. Measurement for a map scale can also be given in *centimeters*, *meters*, or *kilometers*. This type of measurement is called *metric measure*. On some map scales, both standard and metric measure are used.

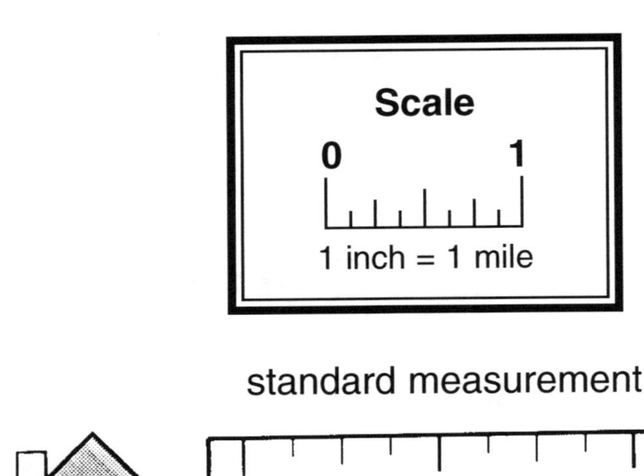

standard measurement

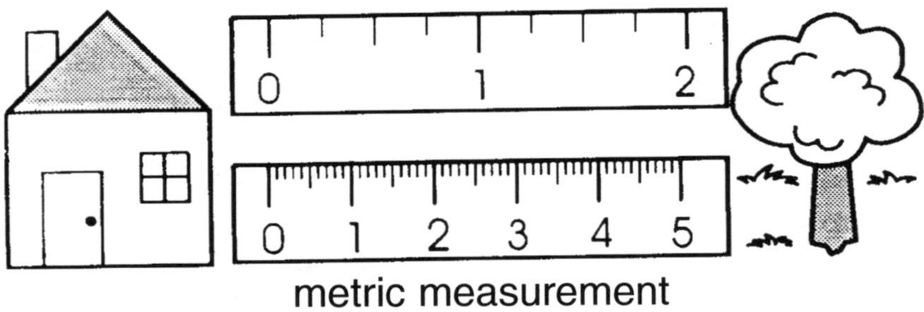

metric measurement

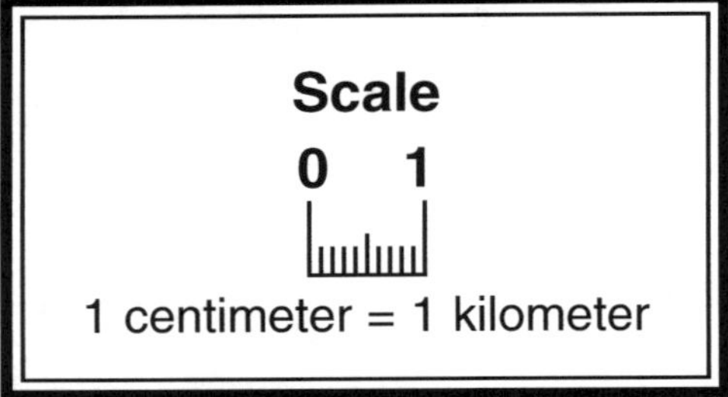

1. How many miles is it from the house to the park?

____

2. How many kilometers is it from the house to the park? _______________________________

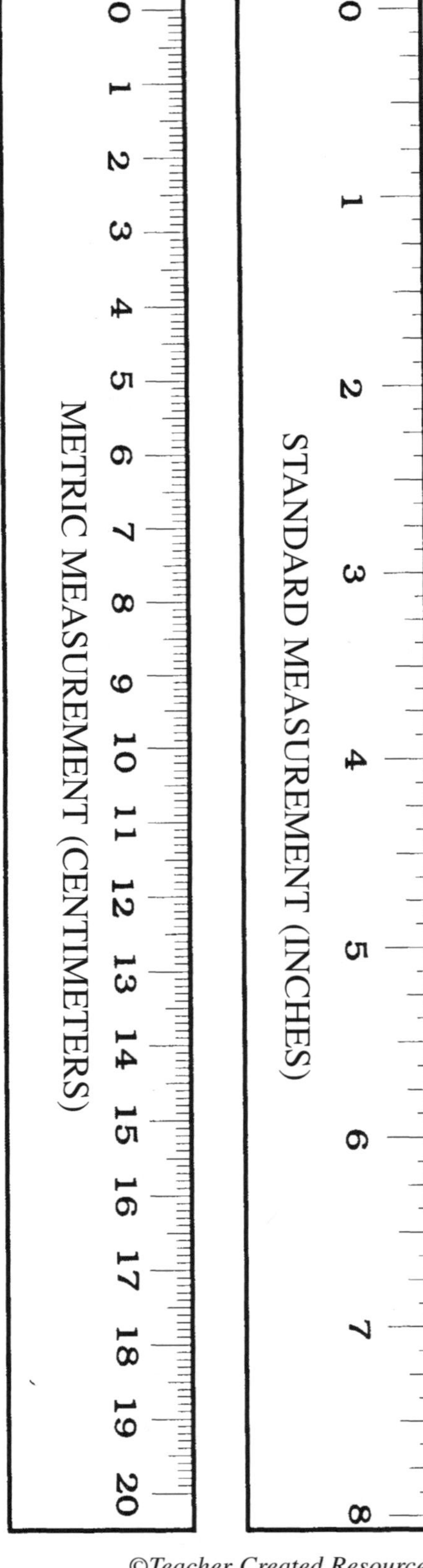

Cut out the rulers on the right side of the page. Use these rulers to help you with standard and metric measurement.

Standard and Metric

What is the distance between the farm houses on this map? Use both your standard and metric rulers for this activity. Measure from dot to dot.

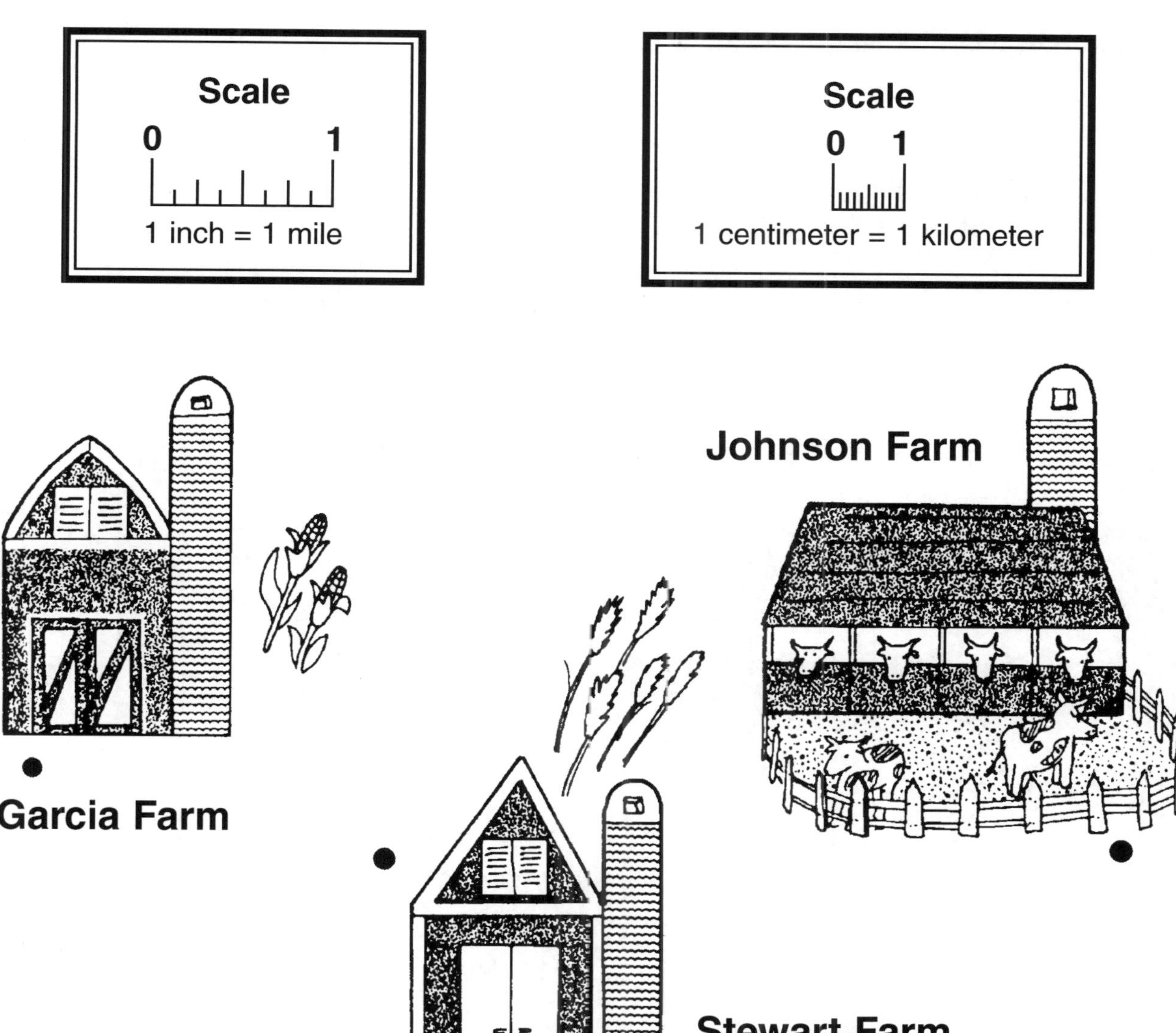

1. How far is the Garcia Farm from the Stewart Farm?

   in miles________________ in kilometers__________________

2. How far is the Garcia Farm from the Johnson Farm?

   in miles ________________ in kilometers__________________

3. How far is the Stewart Farm from the Johnson Farm?

   in miles ________________ in kilometers__________________

Vacation Time!

You and your family have some vacation time. There are five places you would like to go:

1. overnight camping at the ocean
2. a day trip to the county zoo
3. for a picnic at the park
4. to the movie theater
5. on a bike trip to your grandparents' house

Use the map scale and a ruler to find out how far it is from your house to each of these places. Measure from dot to dot.

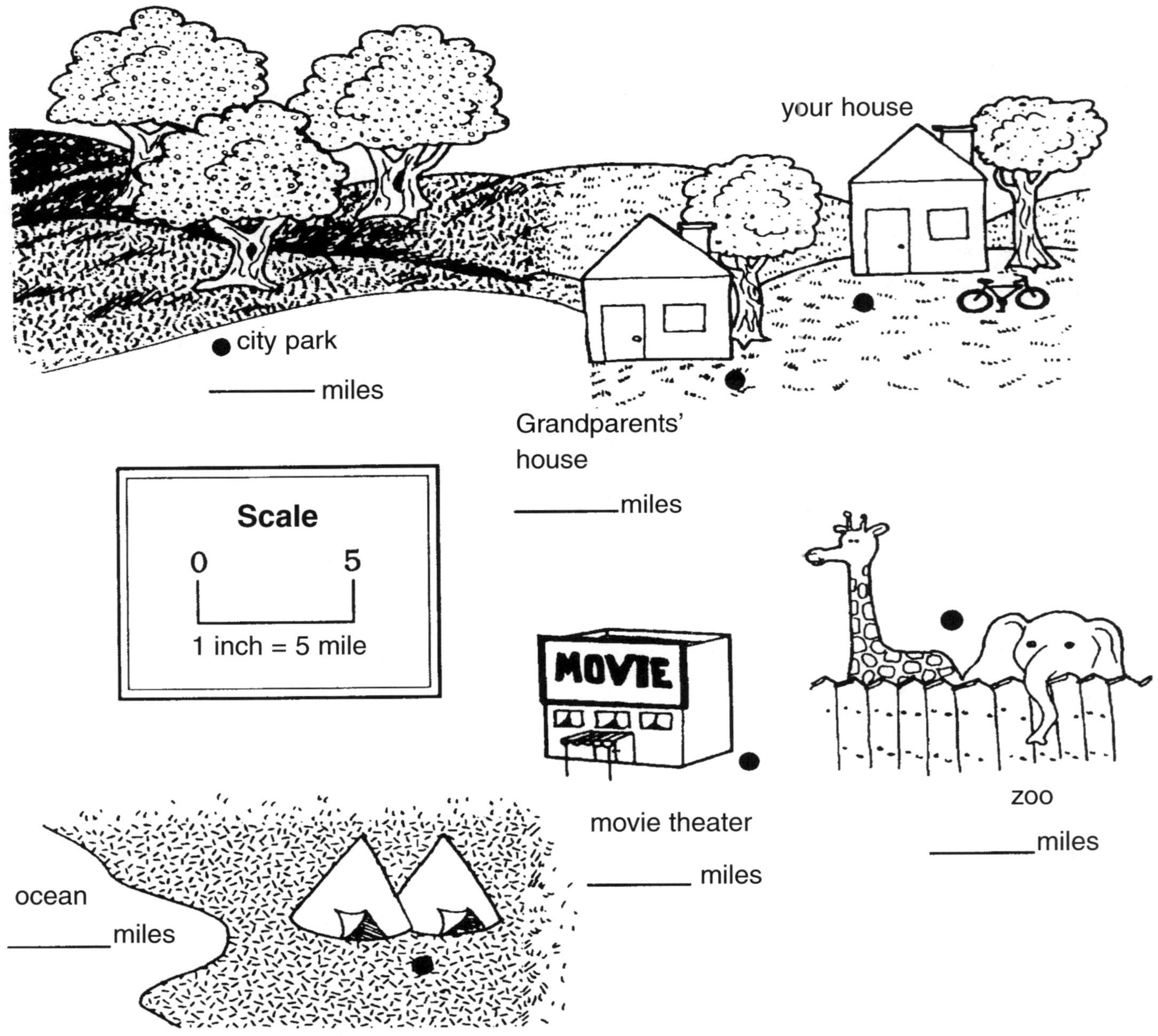

How Far?

Use this map scale and a metric ruler to answer the distance questions on this page.

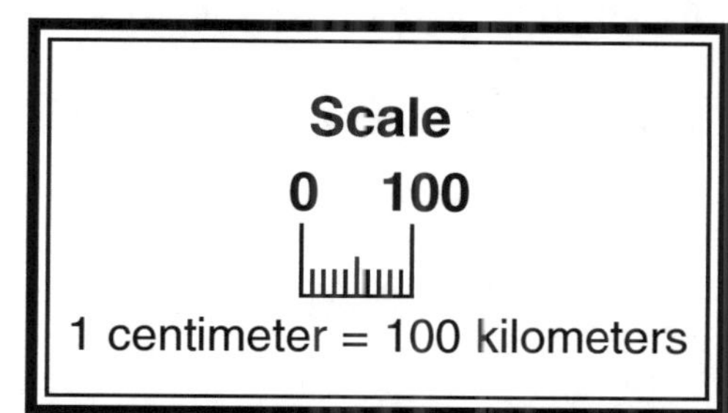

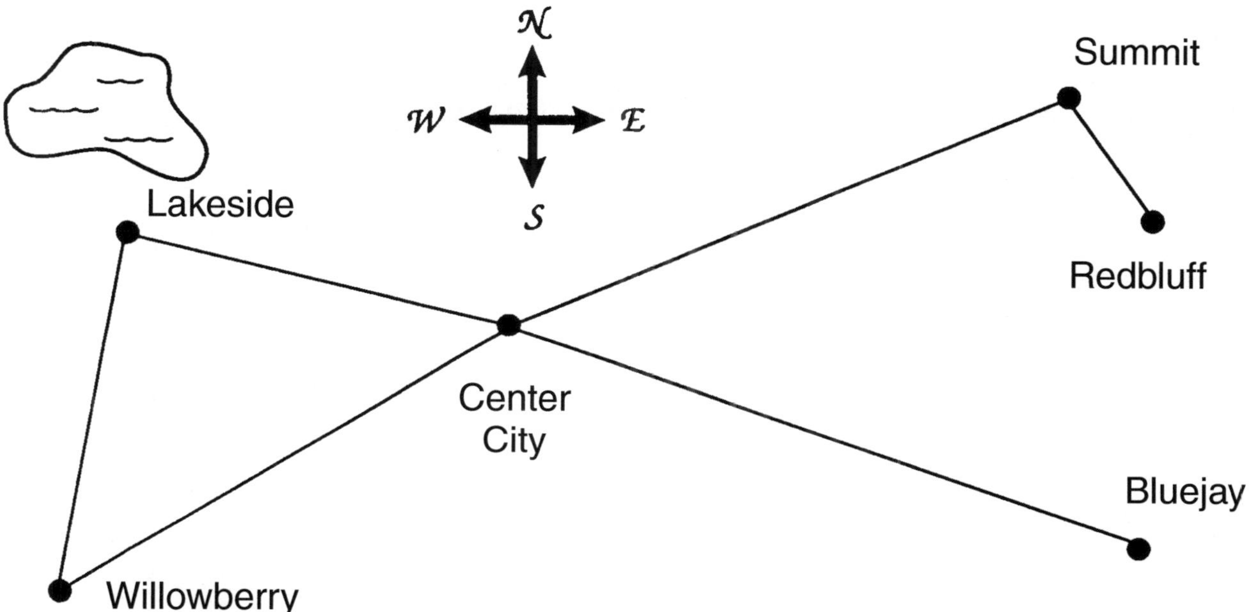

1. Center City is ________________________ kilometers from Bluejay.

2. Summit is ________________________ kilometers from Redbluff.

3. Willowberry is________________________ kilometers from Lakeside.

4. Bluejay is________________________ kilometers from Lakeside.

5. Summit is ________________________ kilometers from Center City.

6. Center City is ________________________ kilometers from Lakeside.

7. Willowberry is________________________ kilometers from Summit.

8. Center City is ________________________ kilometers from Willowberry.

A Trip to the Mountains

You live in Meadowview. You and your family are going to go on a day trip to the mountains and the Natural History Museum. You plan to pick up your cousin, who lives in Oakglen. He is going to join you on your trip and then spend the night at your house.

> *Fill in the blanks below with the help of the map scale and the compass. Trace your trip path as you travel.*

1. You travel ________________ (give direction) for __________ miles to get to your cousin's house.

2. You travel 20 miles southeast to the town of ____________________________.

3. You then drive ___________ miles to the ranger station.

4. Once there, you check in, and take your car up the twisty road to the museum for __________ miles.

5. After a wonderful day, you travel southwest for __________ miles to the town of ___________________. There you have a delicious dinner before heading the __________ miles home to Meadowview.

6. Your trip to the Natural History Museum was __________ miles.

7. Your trip home from the museum was __________ miles.

8. You traveled a total of _______________ miles!

At the Playground

Using metric measurement, answer the questions below the playground map. Give all of your answers in meters. Measure *between the dots*.

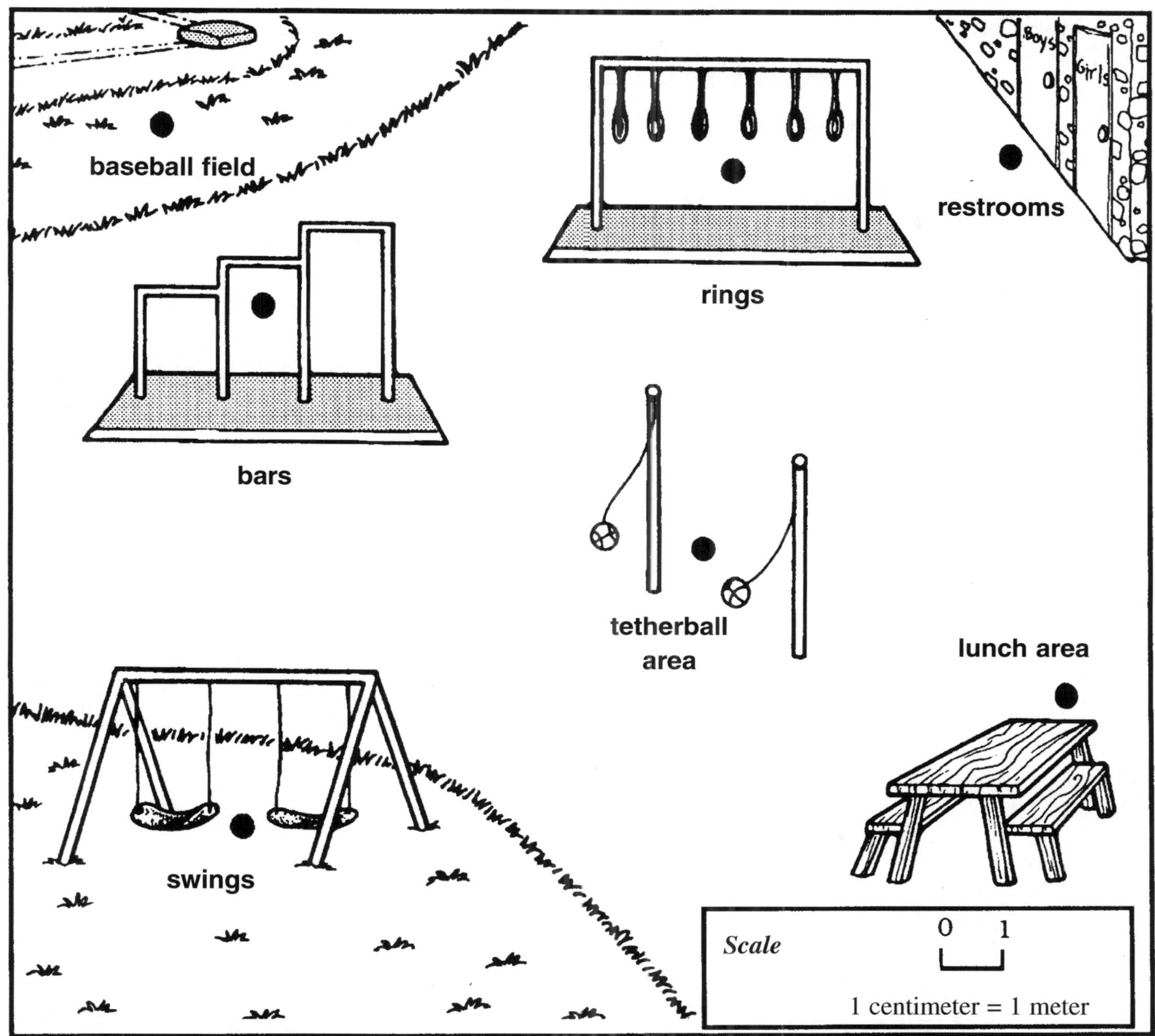

1. How far is it from the swings to the baseball field?________________________

2. How far is it from the rings to the tetherball area?________________________

3. How far is it from the restrooms to the bars?________________________

4. How far is it from the swings to the bars? ________________________

5. How far is it from the baseball field to the lunch area? ________________________

The Title

A *title* is a name. People have titles, and so do pets. Maps also have titles. A map's title tells us what the map is about.

Under each map, write the correct title.

Rivertown	South America
Market Street	My Bedroom

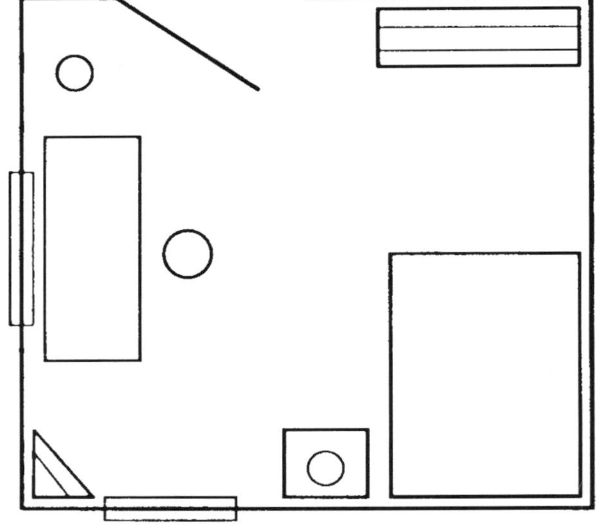

1. __________________________ 2. __________________________

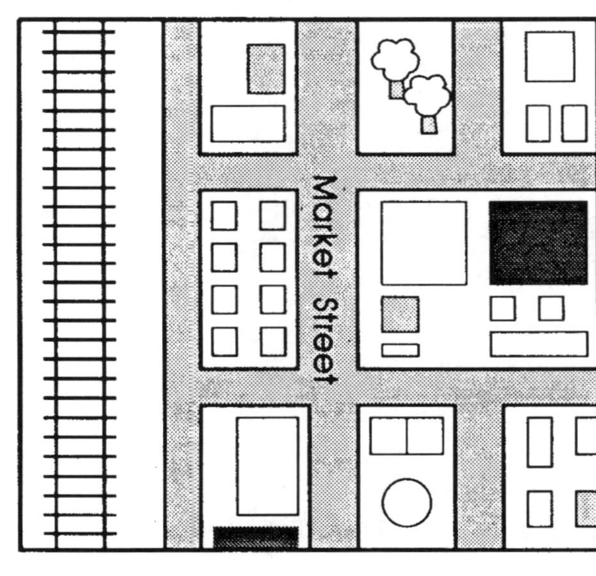

3. __________________________ 4. __________________________

Tell Us More!

A *title* tells us what a map is about. Often, a title can tell us more about the map. A title can tell us what kind of map it is.

There are many kinds of maps. Here are three of them.

* A ***physical map*** tells us something about the shape of the land. It shows where lakes, rivers, mountains, plains, and other "nature-made" things are.

* A ***political map*** shows us cities, capitals, boundaries, and other "human-made" things.

* A ***product map*** shows us what kinds of things are made in and grown on the land.

Look at these maps of Montana and answer the questions below.

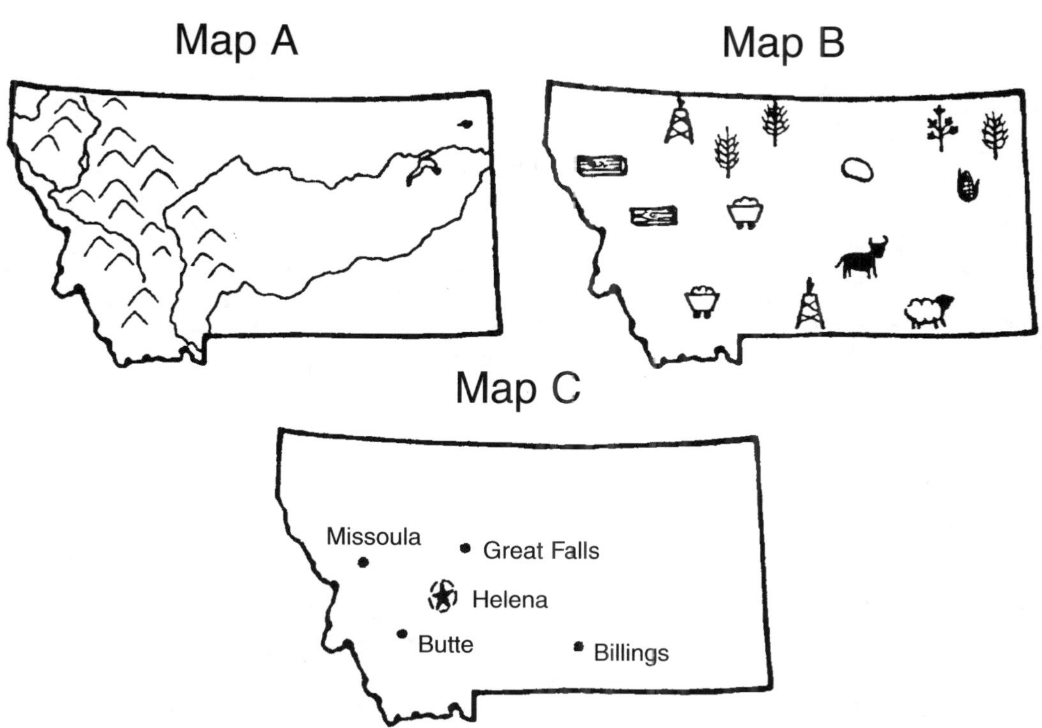

1. Which map is a political map of Montana? ___________________________

2. Which map is a product map of Montana? ___________________________

3. Which map is a physical map of Montana? ___________________________

Titles can help us understand the kinds of maps we use.

Labels

Labels tell us names of places on maps.

> **Read the labels on this County Fair map. Then lightly color each labeled area the color shown in the key.**

Map of the County Fair!

horses	needle-work cooking crafts
pigs sheep	refreshments rest-rooms
poultry cattle	fun zone

horses .... **blue** ☐

pigs .... **pink** ☐

sheep .... **gray** ☐

poultry .... **red** ☐

cattle .... **brown** ☐

needlework .... **orange** ☐

cooking .... **green** ☐

crafts .... **purple** ☐

refreshments .... **white** ☐

restrooms .... **black** ☐

fun zone .... **yellow** ☐

County Fair Color Key

Label These, Please

Write the label of each state under its shape. Use the sentences in the clue box to help you.

Clue Box

Oklahoma looks like it is a pan with a handle.

Idaho looks like a chimney.

Texas is the largest state on this page.

Louisiana looks like a boot.

Michigan has two parts that are separated by water.

Virginia looks like a mountain range.

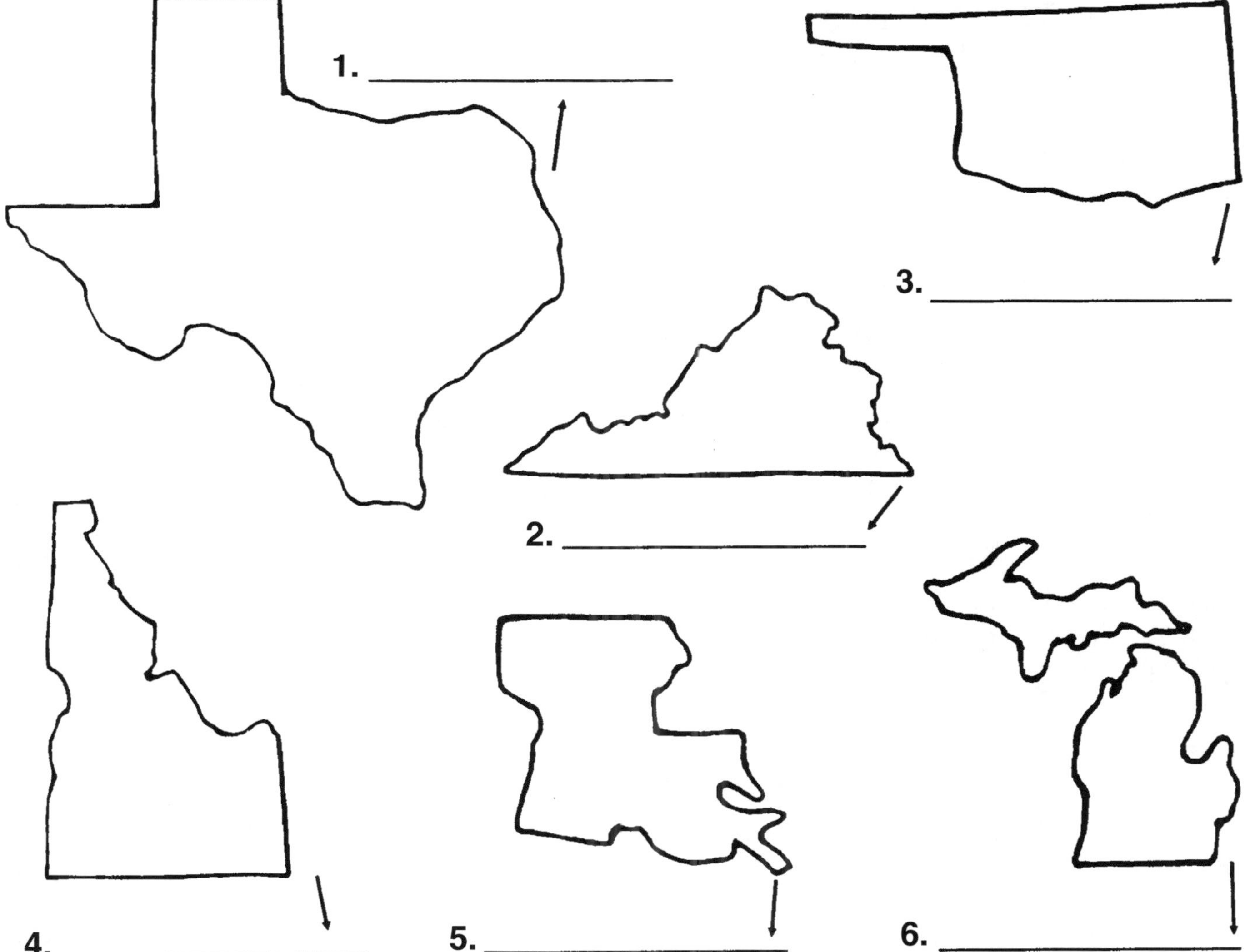

Types of Maps

There are many different types of maps. A map can be drawn of places we see every day, such as our room, our house, or our school. A map can show us the countries, provinces, and states that make up our world. Maps can show us what it looks like inside a building, inside a car, or inside our bodies. There are road maps, airway maps, weather maps, population maps, product maps, and even treasure maps! There are many kinds of maps.

> **Work in small groups to find an example of each of the types of maps on this list. Share what you find with the rest of your class.**

A globe is a model of the Earth that is round like a ball.	1. Find a **globe**.
A map of our solar system would include the sun and the nine planets that orbit the sun.	2. Find a map of our **solar system**.
A relief map shows how high and low the land is.	3. Find a **relief map**.
A city map shows streets, major buildings, parks, and other city things.	4. Find a **city map**.
A boundary is a line that separates states, provinces, countries, and other things that have a dividing line.	5. Find a map that shows the **boundaries** between countries or states.
A product map shows what types of things are raised, grown, or found in a place.	6. Find a **product** map.
A weather map shows the weather of a certain area.	7. Find a **weather** map.

Solar System

A *solar system* is made up of a sun and the planets or other bodies that rotate around it. The solar system we live in is made up of our sun, eight planets, a dwarf planet (Pluto), and other orbiting bodies like moons, comets, and asteroids.

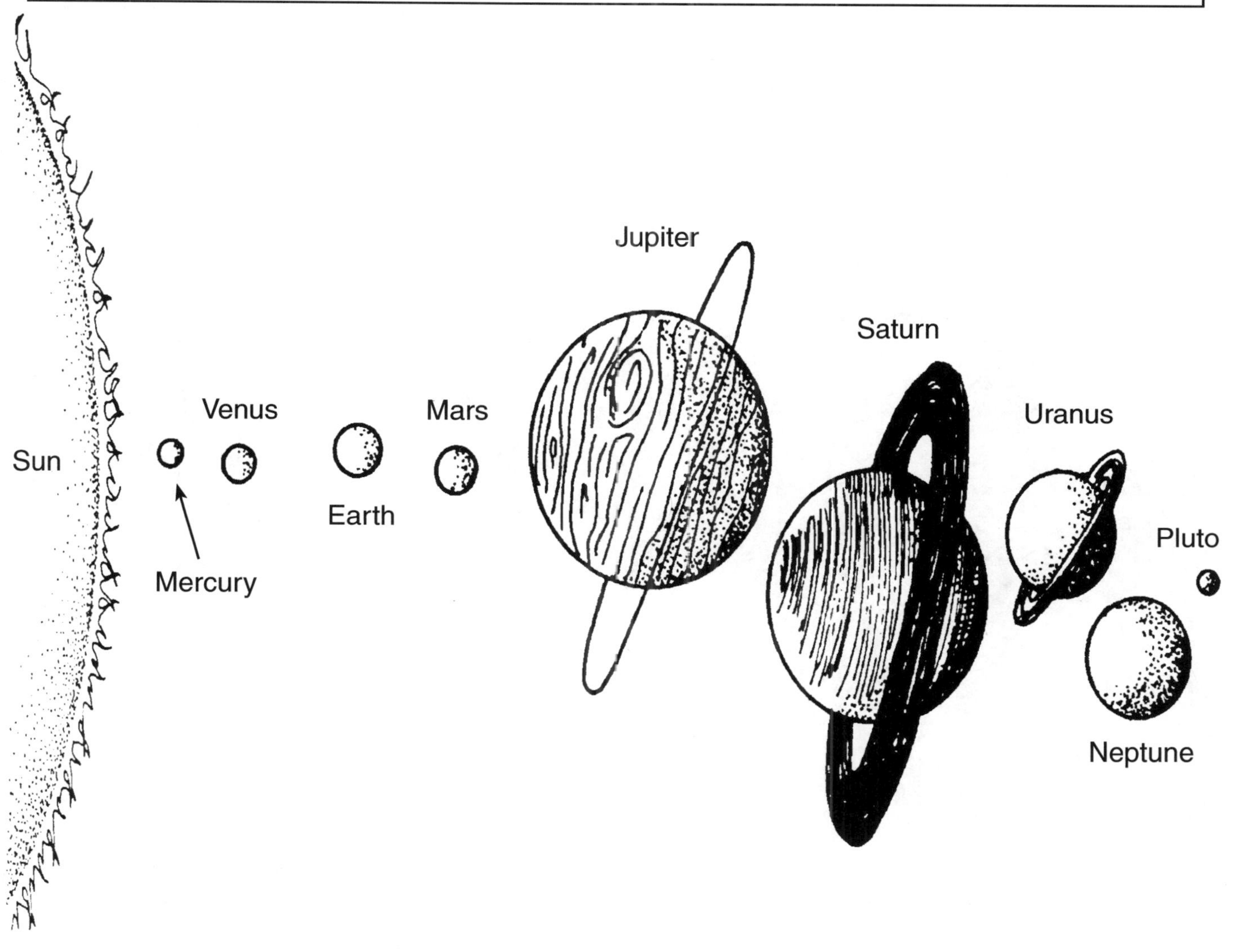

1. _____________________ is the planet that is farthest away from the sun.

2. _____________________ is the largest planet.

3. _____________________ , _____________________ , _____________________ and

_____________________ are larger than the Earth.

4. _____________________ is the planet that is closest to the sun.

5. _____________________ and _____________________ are Earth's nearest planet neighbors.

Continents and Oceans

The largest areas of land in the world are called *continents*. There are seven continents. Which continent do you live on? _______________________________________

The largest areas of water in the world are called *oceans*. There are four main oceans. Which ocean is closest to you?_______________________________________

Color the continents green and the oceans blue.

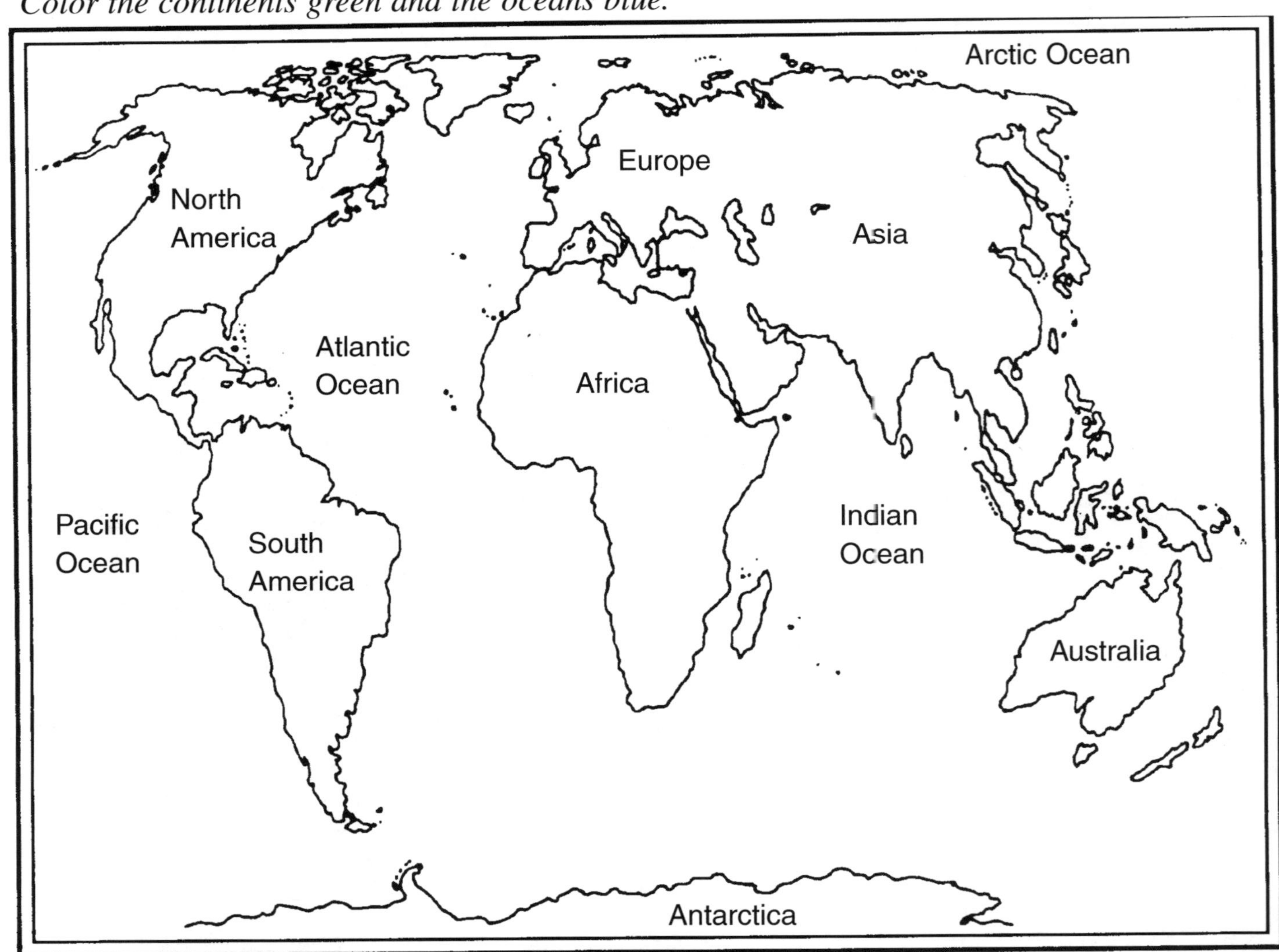

What are the names of the seven continents?

1. _______________   2. _______________   3. _______________

4. _______________   5. _______________   6. _______________

7. _______________

What are the names of the four major oceans?

1. _______________   2. _______________

3. _______________   4. _______________

Swim or Walk?

Look at this map of the continents and oceans of the world. If you were on each of the numbered areas, would you swim or walk?

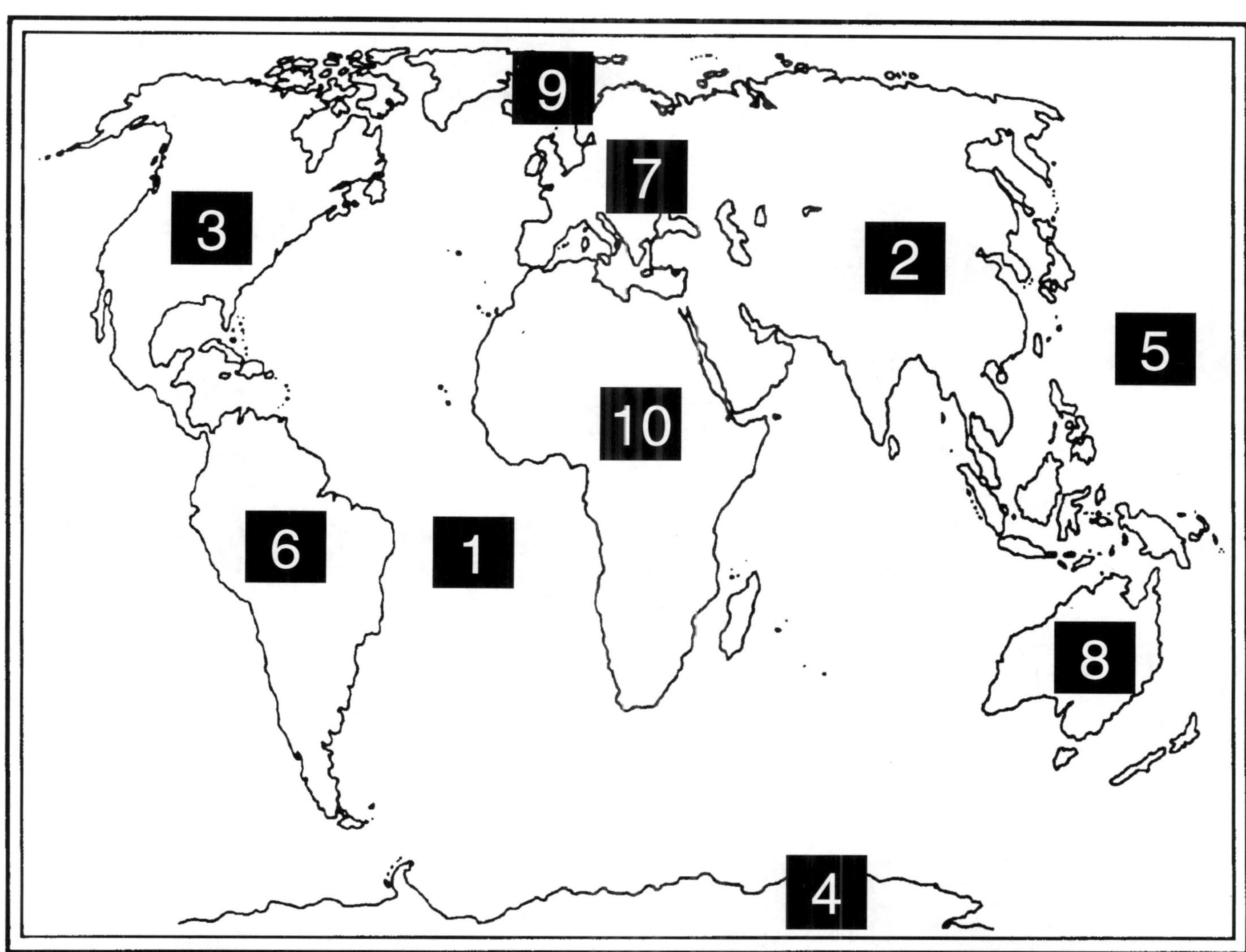

Write *swim* or *walk* here.

1. _____________ 2. _____________ 3. _____________ 4._____________ 5. _____________

6. _____________ 7. _____________ 8. _____________ 9. _____________ 10. _____________

Use the world map on page 46 to help you correctly label the continents and oceans on this map. Then color the continents green and the oceans blue.

Globes

The Earth is round, not flat. Even though flat maps can show different parts of our planet, a globe gives us a truer picture of what the Earth is really like. A *globe* is a model of the Earth. It is round like the Earth is round. A globe can rotate like the Earth rotates.

Color the water blue and the land green. Then answer these questions.

1. What do we have to do to see Asia, Europe, and Africa? _______________________

____

2. Which is more like the Earth, a flat map or a globe? _______________________

Why? ____

____

The Equator and Hemispheres

The Earth is divided into two parts by an imaginary line called the *equator*. The part of the Earth that is north of the equator is called the *Northern Hemisphere*. The part of the Earth that is south of the equator is called the *Southern Hemisphere*. A *sphere* is a globe or other ball shape. The Earth is sphere. A *hemisphere* is half of a sphere.

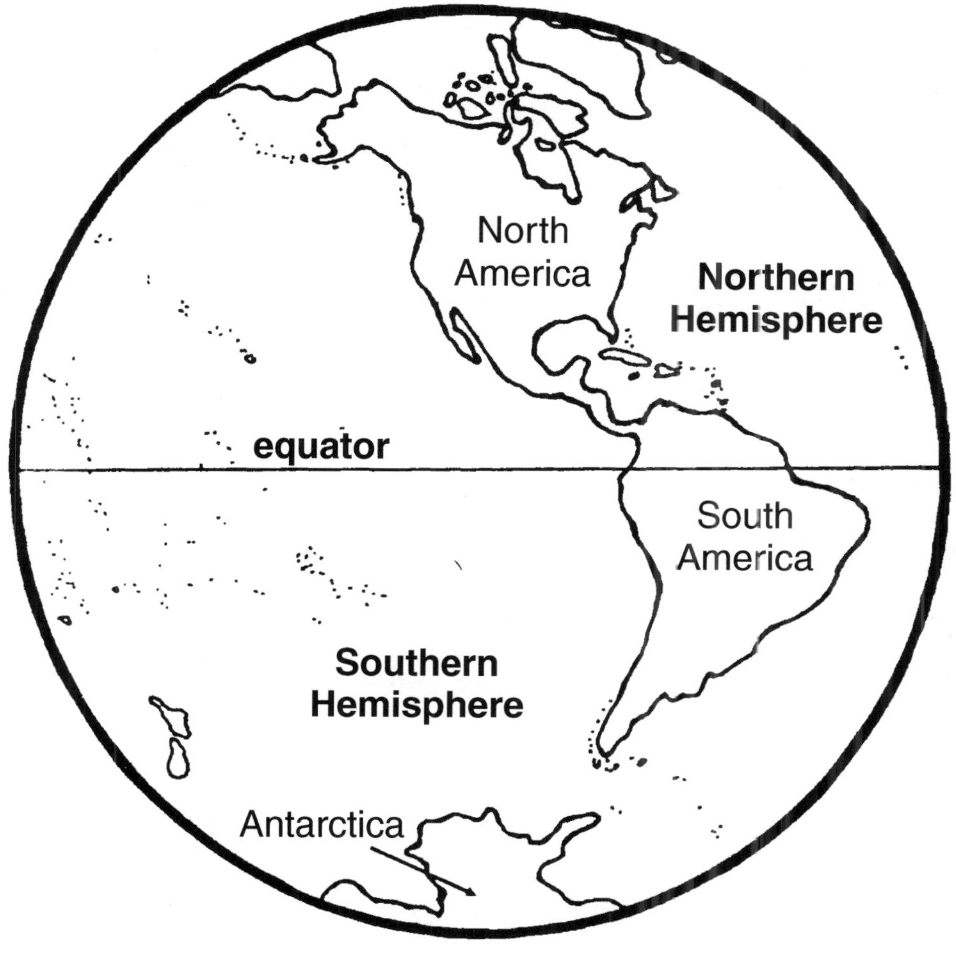

The equator is like an imaginary cut that divides the sphere of the Earth into two half-spheres, or hemispheres.

1. Trace the equator with a blue crayon.

2. Color the Northern Hemisphere green.

3. Color the Southern Hemisphere yellow.

4. What continent on this map is in the Northern Hemisphere?

____

5. What continent on this map is divided by the equator? ____________________

____

6. What continent on this map is completely in the Southern Hemisphere?

____

The Poles and Hemispheres

Just like the Earth is divided into north and south halves by the equator, it is also divided into east and west halves by an imaginary line running from the North Pole to the South Pole. The line divides the Earth into the Western Hemisphere and the Eastern Hemisphere.

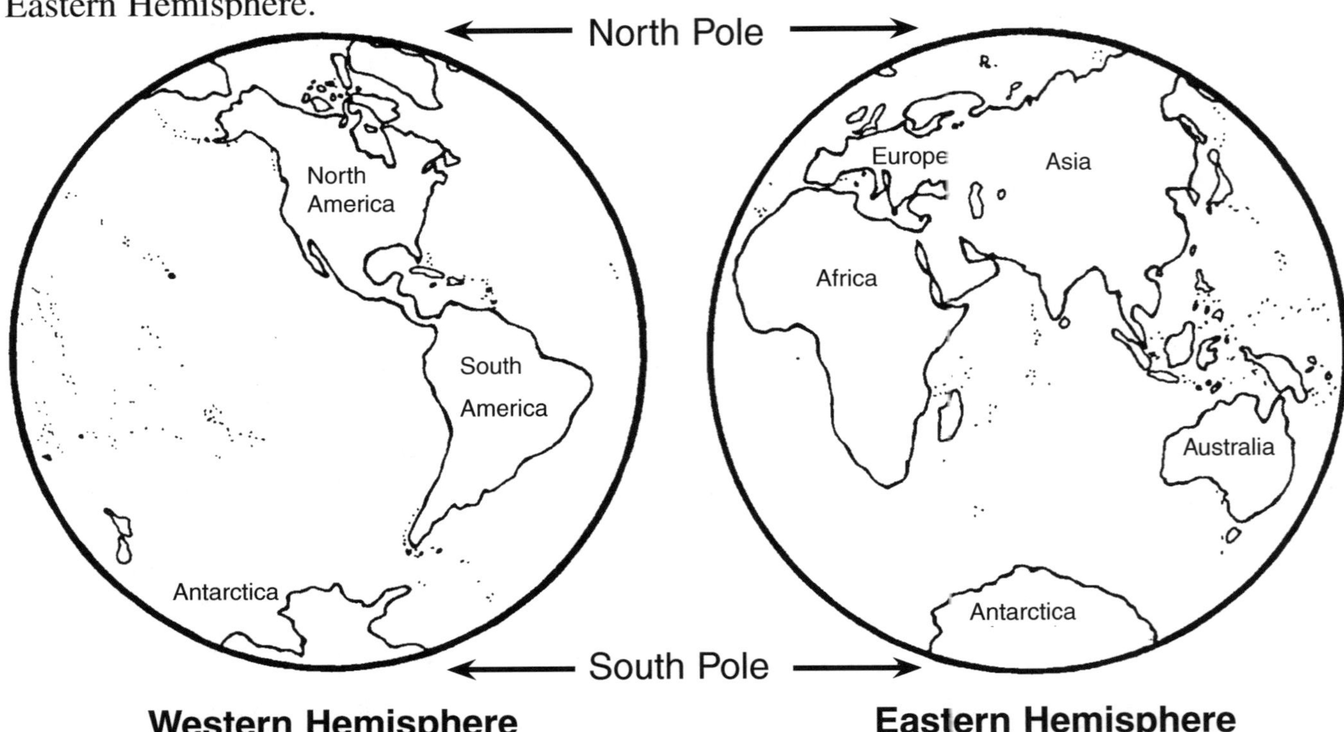

1. Color the Western Hemisphere a light color.

2. Color the Eastern Hemisphere a different light color.

3. Name the continents in the Western Hemisphere.

     1. _______________________________

     2. _______________________________

     3. _______________________________

4. Name the continents that are in the Eastern Hemisphere.

     1. _____________________   4._____________________

     2. _____________________   5._____________________

     3. _____________________

5. Name the continent that is in both Western and Eastern Hemispheres.

Which Slice of the World?

Use these maps of the Earth and its hemispheres to help you answer the questions at the bottom of the page.

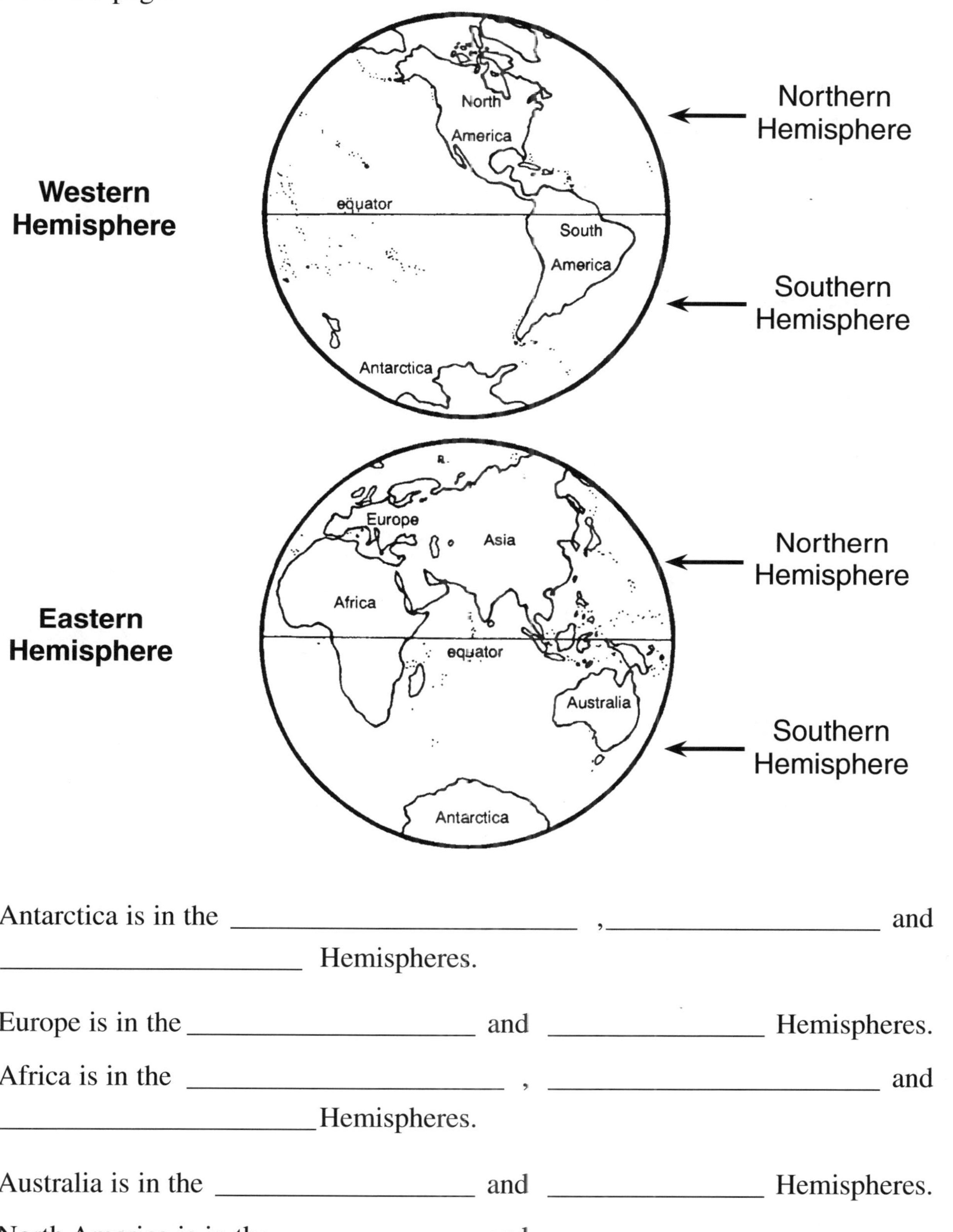

1. Antarctica is in the ______________________ , ______________________ and ______________________ Hemispheres.

2. Europe is in the ______________________ and ______________________ Hemispheres.

3. Africa is in the ______________________ , ______________________ and ______________________ Hemispheres.

4. Australia is in the ______________________ and ______________________ Hemispheres.

5. North America is in the ______________ and ______________________ ______________________ Hemispheres.

Landforms

Some maps show where lakes and rivers are. They also show mountains, valleys, plains, and plateaus. Maps that show the form of the land are called *landform* maps.

Read this map. Then follow the directions at the bottom of the page. Here are some definitions to help you.

lake = enclosed body of water

river = running water in a path that has cut the land

plateau = high, flat land

mountain = high, steep-sided land

valley = land that is much lower than the land around it

plain = open, flat land, lower than a plateau

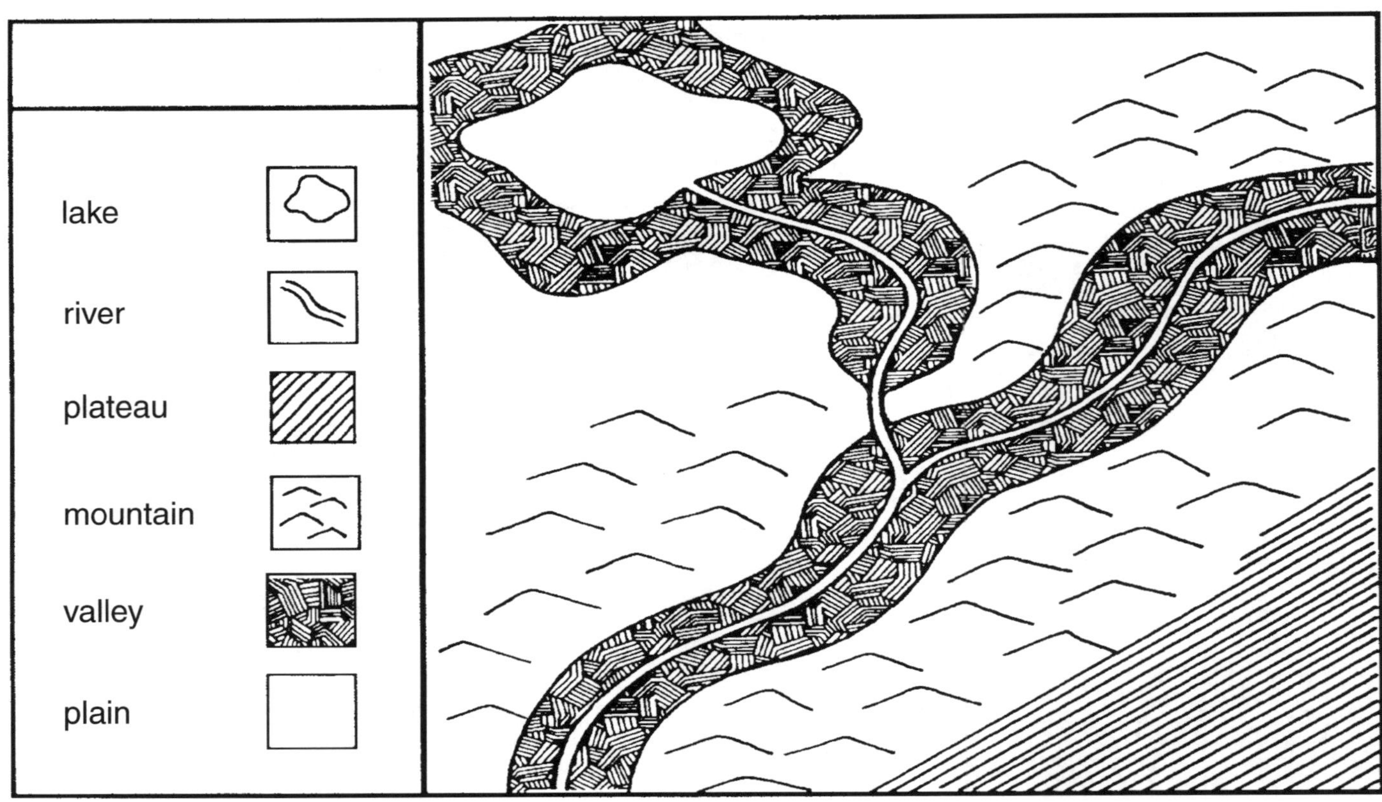

Color the lakes blue.	Color the mountains brown.
Color the rivers blue.	Color the valleys green.
Color the plateaus tan.	Color the plains yellow.

Find One, Make One

Use an encyclopedia or other reference to find a map that shows different landforms.

Resource I used: ____

(Write name of reference)

Page number: _____________

I found a map of this place: _______________________________________

The landforms I found on this map were: _____________________________

____

Share your map with your class.

In the box on this page, create your own landform map. Be sure to create a clear key using symbols and colors. Then cut out your landform map and put it on a class bulletin board.

Landform Key

Student's name:

What a Relief!

Sometimes maps are made where you can *feel* the highness and lowness of the land. These landform maps are called *relief* maps. Plastic, clay, or another moldable substance is used to create the mountains, valleys, and plains of the land.

> ## *Work with a partner to create your own relief map!*

1. Decide the place you want to map in relief form. It may be a real or imagined place.

2. Use a piece of heavy tag or a lightweight board as your map base.

3. Draw the shape of your place on your map base. Mark the spots certain landforms will be. Create a key for the landforms.

4. Use modeling dough, clay, or other teacher-supplied material to begin forming your mountains, plateaus, highlands, and other spots above board level.

5. Draw in lakes, rivers, valleys, and other "low" spots.

6. After your relief map dries, paint your landforms and identify them in your key.

Boundaries

Here is part of the United States. Five states can be found within this shape. Do you know any of them?

This time, lines have been drawn to show where one state ends and another state begins.

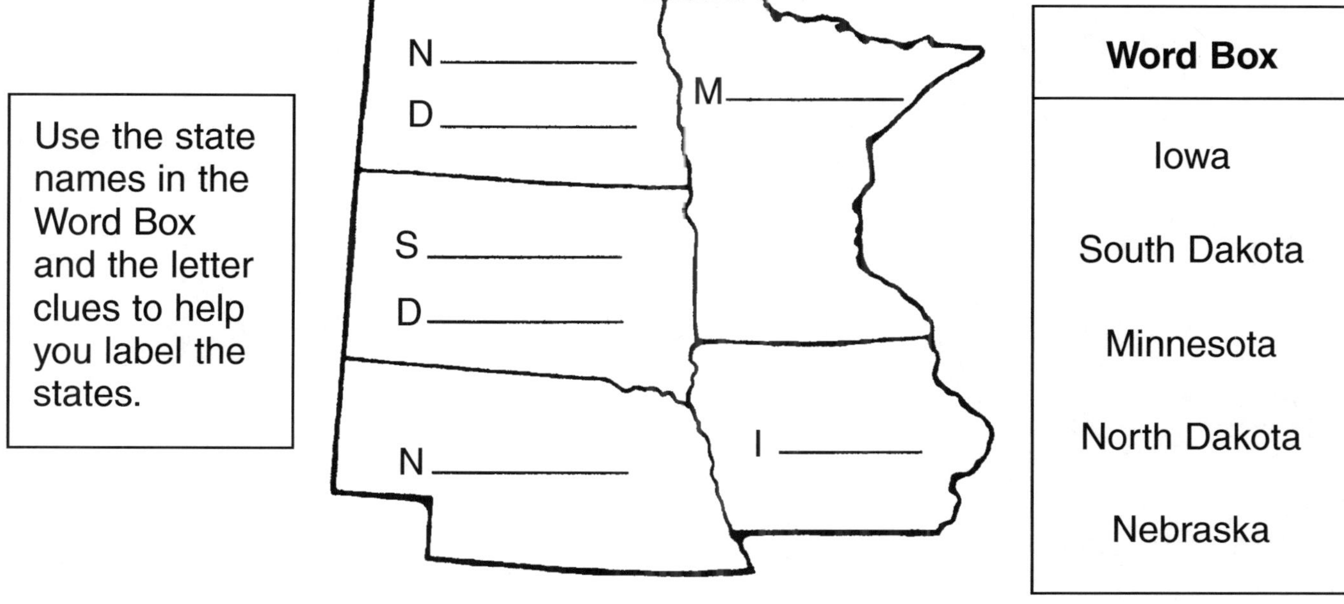

Use the state names in the Word Box and the letter clues to help you label the states.

The lines that show the dividing lines between countries, provinces, states, and counties are called *boundary lines*.

North American Boundaries

On this map are three of the countries in North America.

- Make the boundary between Canada and the United States blue.
- Make the boundary between Mexico and the United States red.
- Color Canada gold, the United States purple, and Mexico green.

Canada

[ ] gold

United States

[ ] purple

Mexico

[ ] green

CanYou Find It?

This is the country of Canada. The boundary lines show each of the provinces and territories that make up Canada. But the mapmaker forgot to label all of the provinces.

Use a map of Canada to help you label the missing provinces: Ontario, Alberta, British Columbia, and Quebec.

Write each province name in its correct place. Then color each Canadian province or territory a different color.

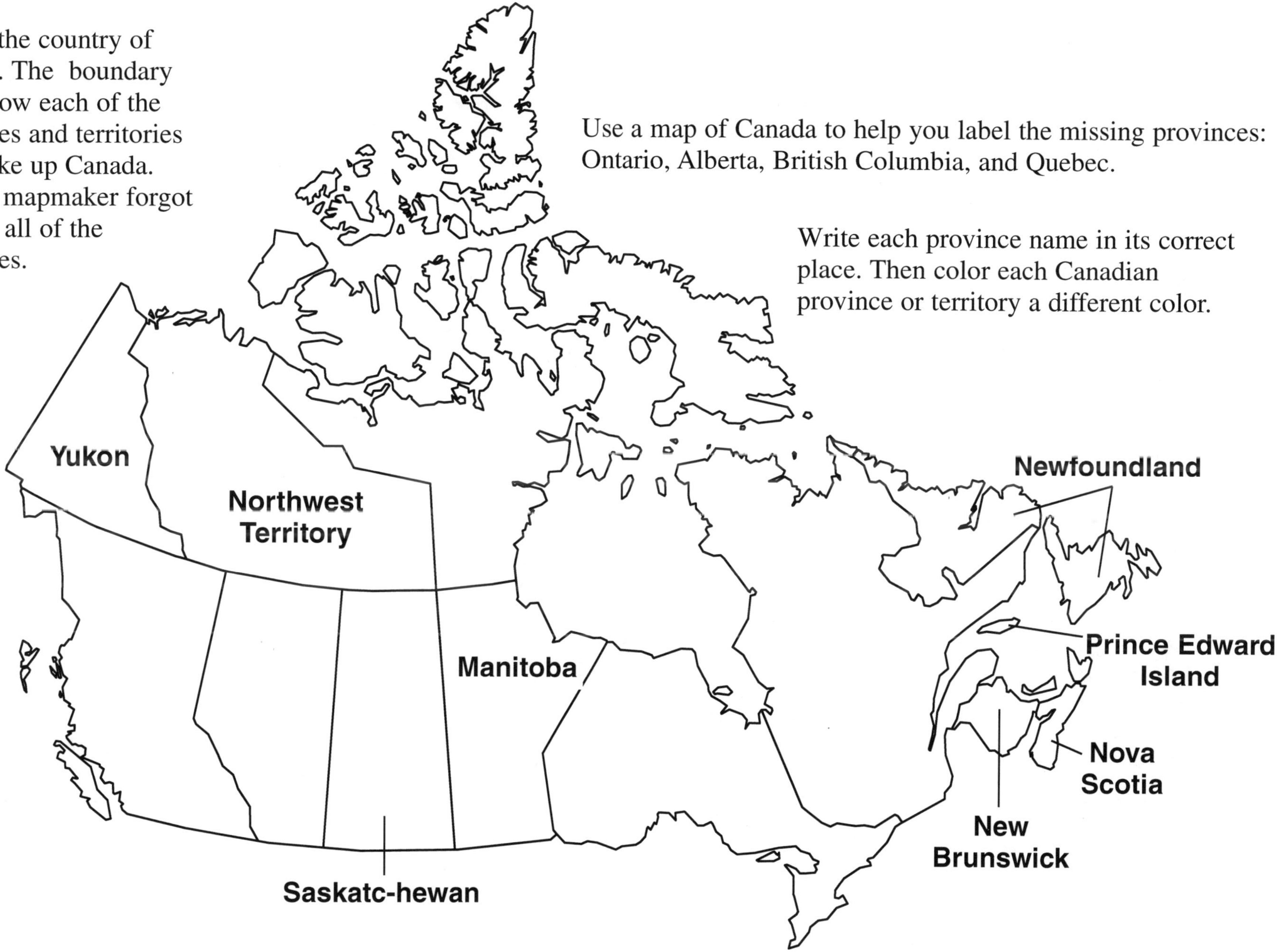

By the Color!

Here are the boundary lines of the states in the United States.

Color the 50 states of the United States any colors you choose. Stay in the boundary lines as you color.

Do not color any states that touch each other the same color!

In Mexico

Mexico was not always the size it is today. In the 1800s, Mexico was much larger. But in 1845 and 1848, two parts of Mexico became part of the United States. And in 1853, the United States bought a part of Mexico for ten million dollars.

Read this map, looking carefully at the boundary lines.

- Outline the old boundary lines of Mexico in red.
- Outline the present boundary lines of Mexico in purple.
- Color the 1853 change yellow.
- Color the 1848 land change orange.
- Color the 1845 land change green.

Your Boundaries!

Boundary lines are dividing lines between places. Countries have boundary lines, states have boundary lines, provinces and territories have boundary lines.

Do you have boundary lines? Are there places you can and cannot go?

Complete this boundary line survey.

1. Are there any places in your home you are not allowed to go unless you have permission? *(For example, a brother or sister's room, a parent's work area, etc.)*

   ____

   ____

2. Are there any places in your yard you are not allowed to go unless you have permission? *(For example, a swimming pool or hot tub area, under a porch or deck, etc.)*

   ____

   ____

3. Are there any places in your school you are not allowed to go unless you have permission? *(For example, a machinery or equipment area, the teachers' lunchroom, etc.)*

   ____

   ____

4. How far are you allowed to go by yourself on the street where you live?

   ____

   ____

5. How far are you allowed to go by yourself in your neighborhood?

   ____

   ____

On the back of this paper, draw a map of your house, yard, school, street, or neighborhood. Draw in your boundary lines on this map using a brightly colored marker or crayon.

Grids

A *grid* is a group of lines drawn a special way. This group of lines makes blocks. Numbers and letters are used on the grid to help you name blocks.

You can find something on a grid by putting a finger of your right hand on a number and a finger of your left hand on a letter. Then slide your fingers toward each other until they meet.

Try it! What is in block A3?

____

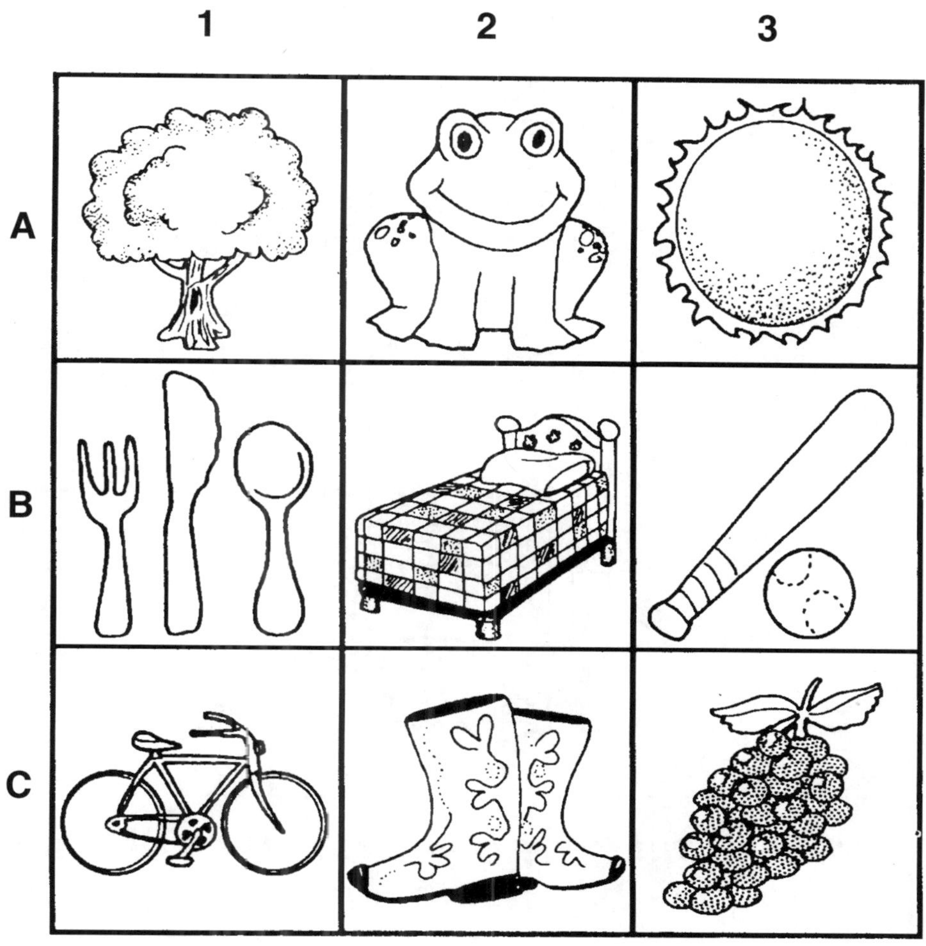

Use the grid to answer these questions.

1. What is in block C1? _______________________

2. What is in block B2? _______________________

3. What is in block C2?_______________________

4. What is in block A1?_______________________

5. What is in block B3? _______________________

6. In what block are the fork, knife, and spoon? _______________________

7. In what block are the grapes? _______________________

8. In what block is the frog?_______________________

On the Playground

A grid can help you find places on a map. Here is a map of a school playground.

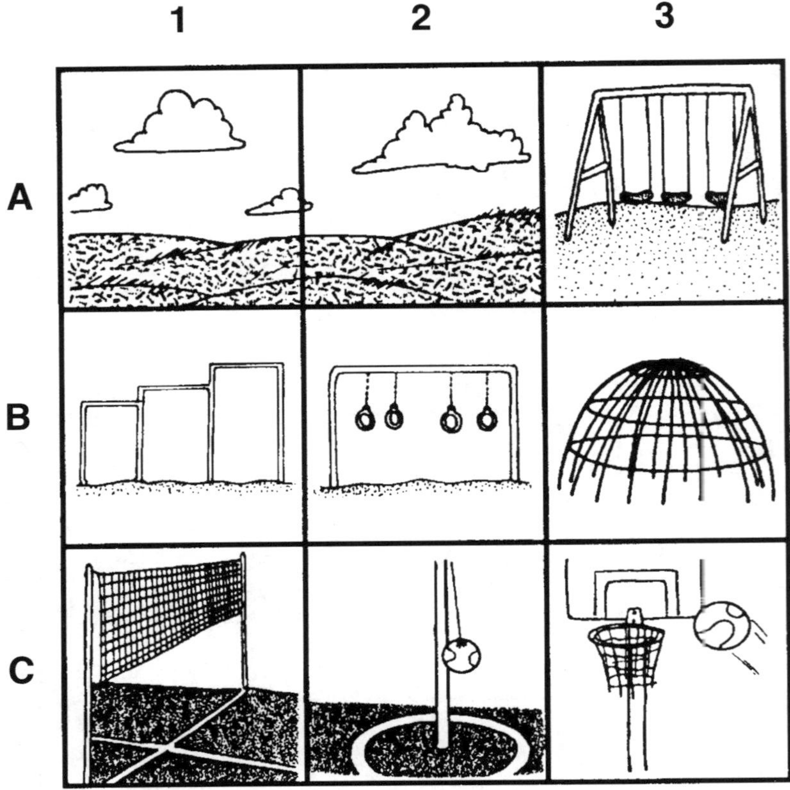

Use this grid to help you answer these questions. Put the letter before the number when you answer.

1. In what block are the swings?_____________________ Color this block red.

2. In what block are the bars? _____________________ Color this block yellow.

3. In what block are the rings? _____________________ Color this block orange.

4. In what block is the basketball hoop?_____________________ Color this block purple.

5. In what two blocks are the grass fields?_____________________ Color these blocks green.

6. In what block is the tetherball? _____________________ Color this block blue.

7. In what block is the climbing gym? _____________________ Color this block pink.

8. In what block is the volleyball net? _____________________ Color this block brown.

In the City

Use the grid on this city map to find the places listed at the bottom of the page.

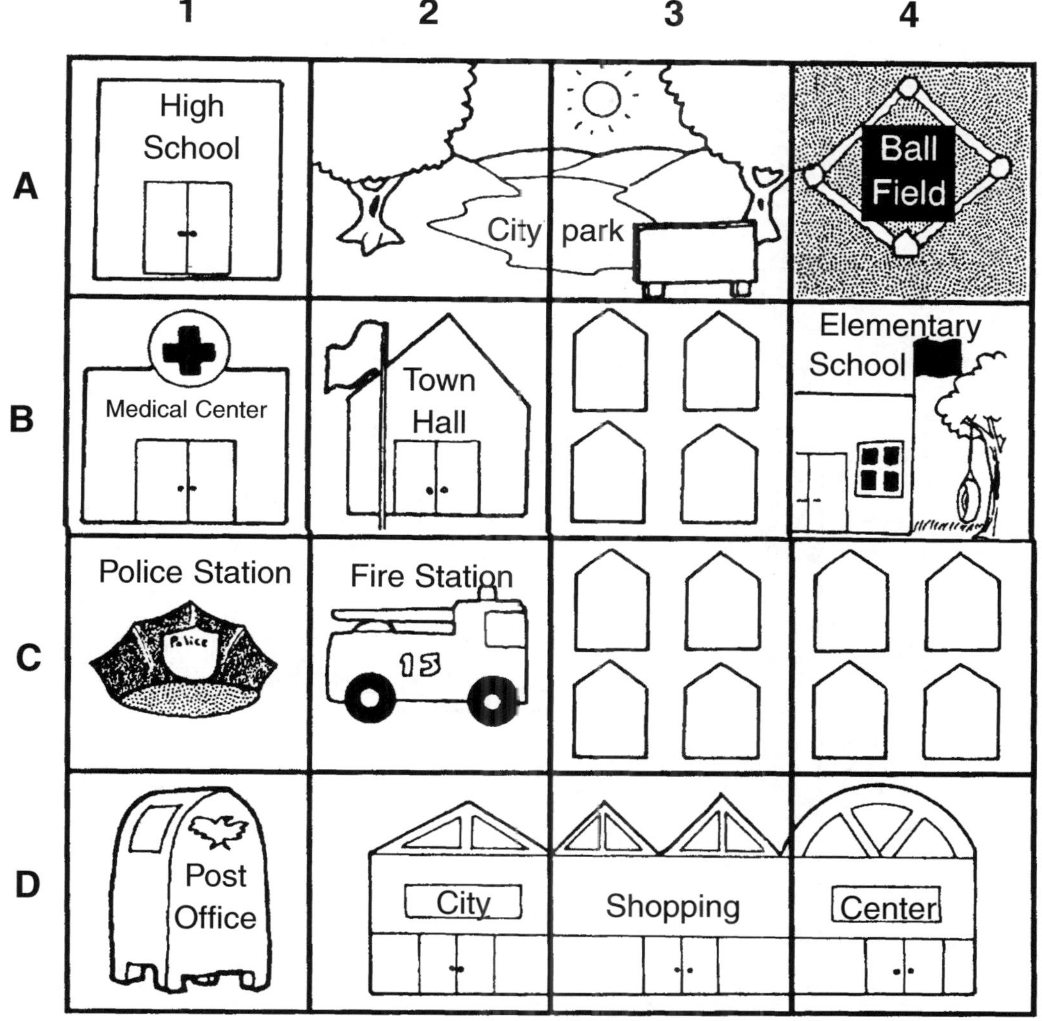

Write the letter before the number for each place you find.

1. High School _______________________

2. Fire Station _______________________

3. Ball Field _______________________

4. Town Hall _______________________

5. City Park ____**A2**____ and________

6. City Shopping Center __________ ,

____**D3**____ , and___________

7. Elementary School _____________

8. Police Station _______________

9. Post Office_________________

10. Medical Center _______________

Across and Down

Use what you know about grids to complete this map.

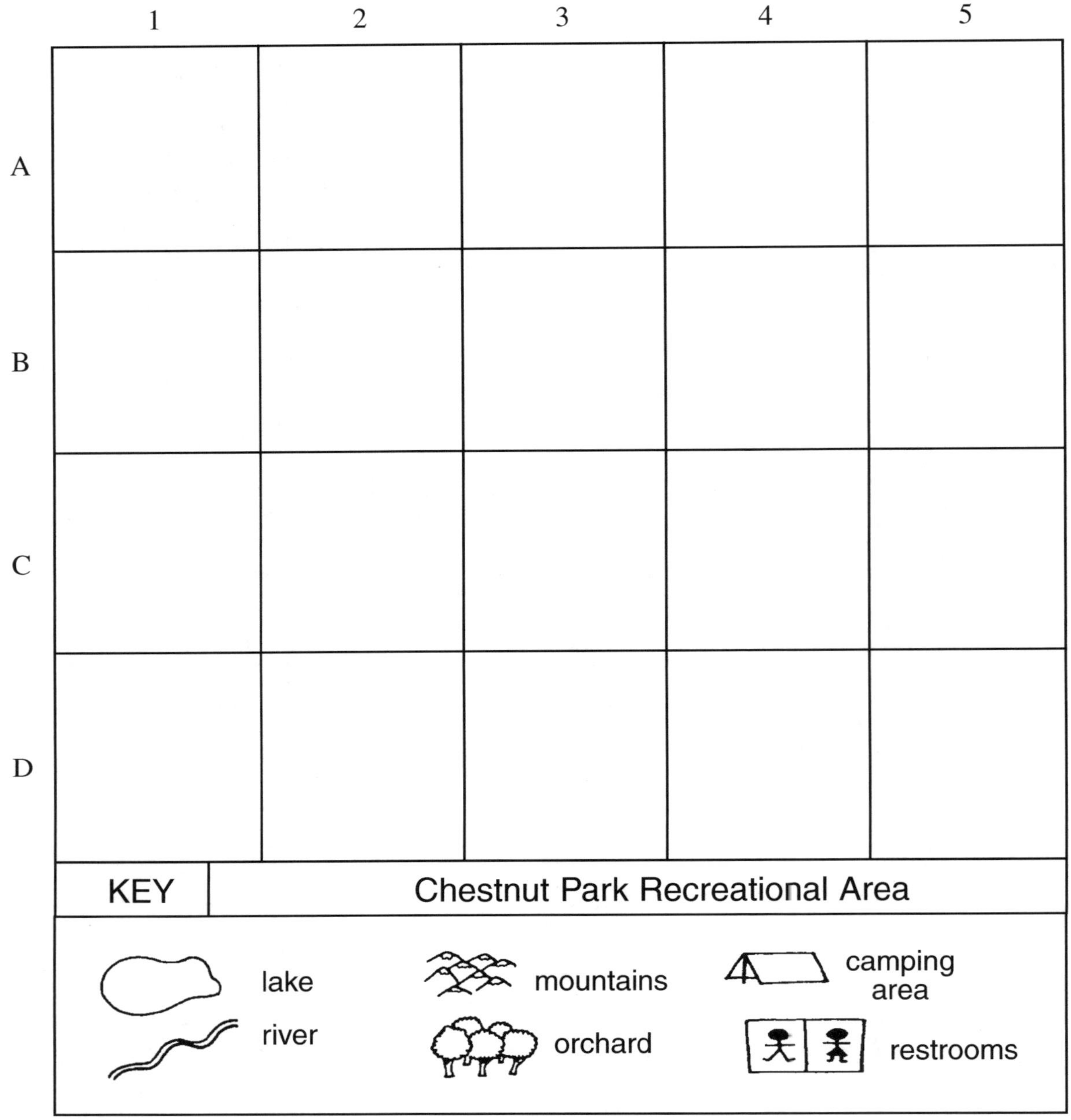

<table>
<tr><td></td><td>1</td><td>2</td><td>3</td><td>4</td><td>5</td></tr>
<tr><td>A</td><td></td><td></td><td></td><td></td><td></td></tr>
<tr><td>B</td><td></td><td></td><td></td><td></td><td></td></tr>
<tr><td>C</td><td></td><td></td><td></td><td></td><td></td></tr>
<tr><td>D</td><td></td><td></td><td></td><td></td><td></td></tr>
</table>

KEY	Chestnut Park Recreational Area

- lake
- river
- mountains
- orchard
- camping area
- restrooms

1. Draw a lake that covers part of B2, B3, C2, and C3.

2. Draw a river that begins in D1 and ends in the lake.

3. Draw mountains in A5, B5, and C5.

4. Draw an orchard in D2 and D3.

5. Draw camping areas in A1, A2, C1, C4, and D4.

6. Draw a restroom in B4.

Road Maps

A *road map* helps people who drive get from place to place. *Road maps* show different types of roads, the distances from town to town, scenic routes, rest areas, and many other things.

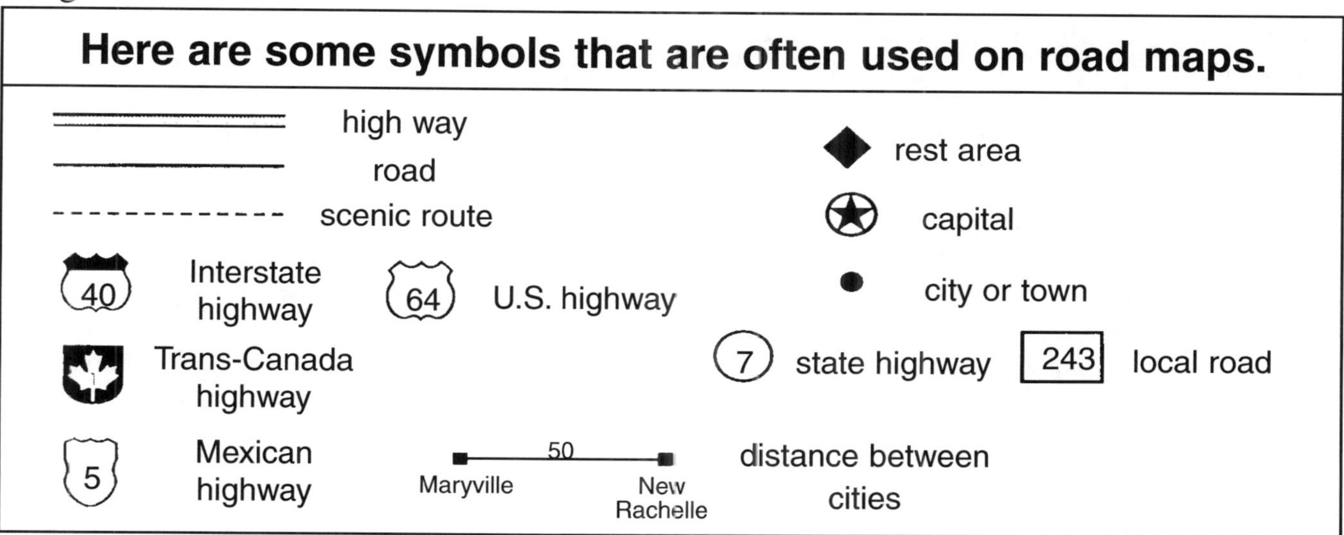

Read this map. Then answer the questions at the bottom of the page.

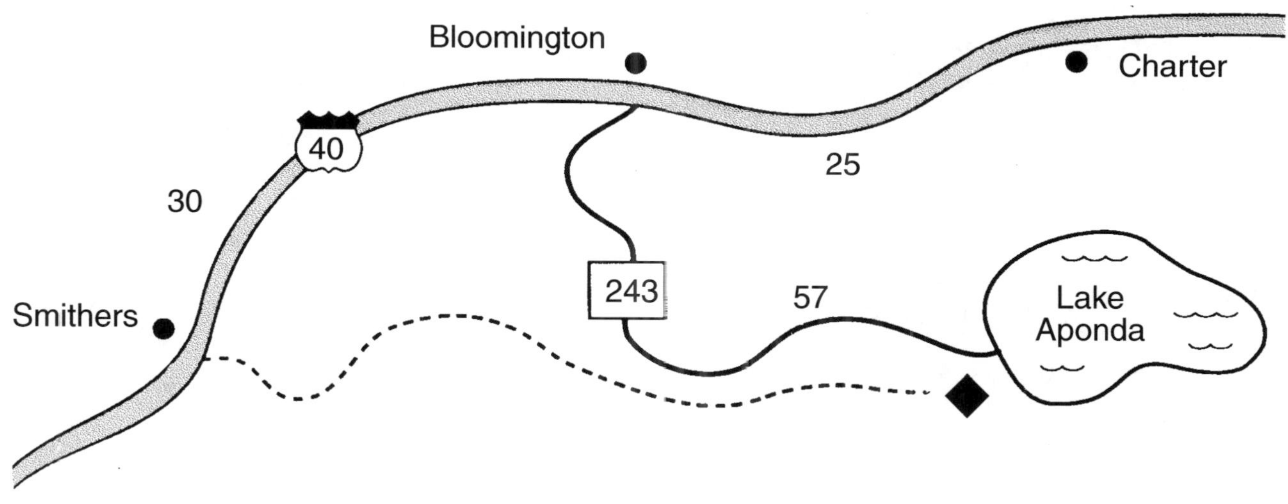

1. Interstate Highway 40 passes through what cities?

   _________________ , _________________ , and _________________

2. What road leads from Bloomington to Lake Aponda? _________________

3. How many miles is it from:

   Bloomington to Charter?____

   Smithers to Bloomington? ____

   Bloomington to Lake Aponda?______________________________________

4. A scenic route leads from the Lake Aponda rest area to what city?

   ____

Drive Away!

You are all ready to go on a trip with your family to Seabreeze Beach. Your father and mother have asked you to be in charge of reading the map.

Use this map to answer the questions below.

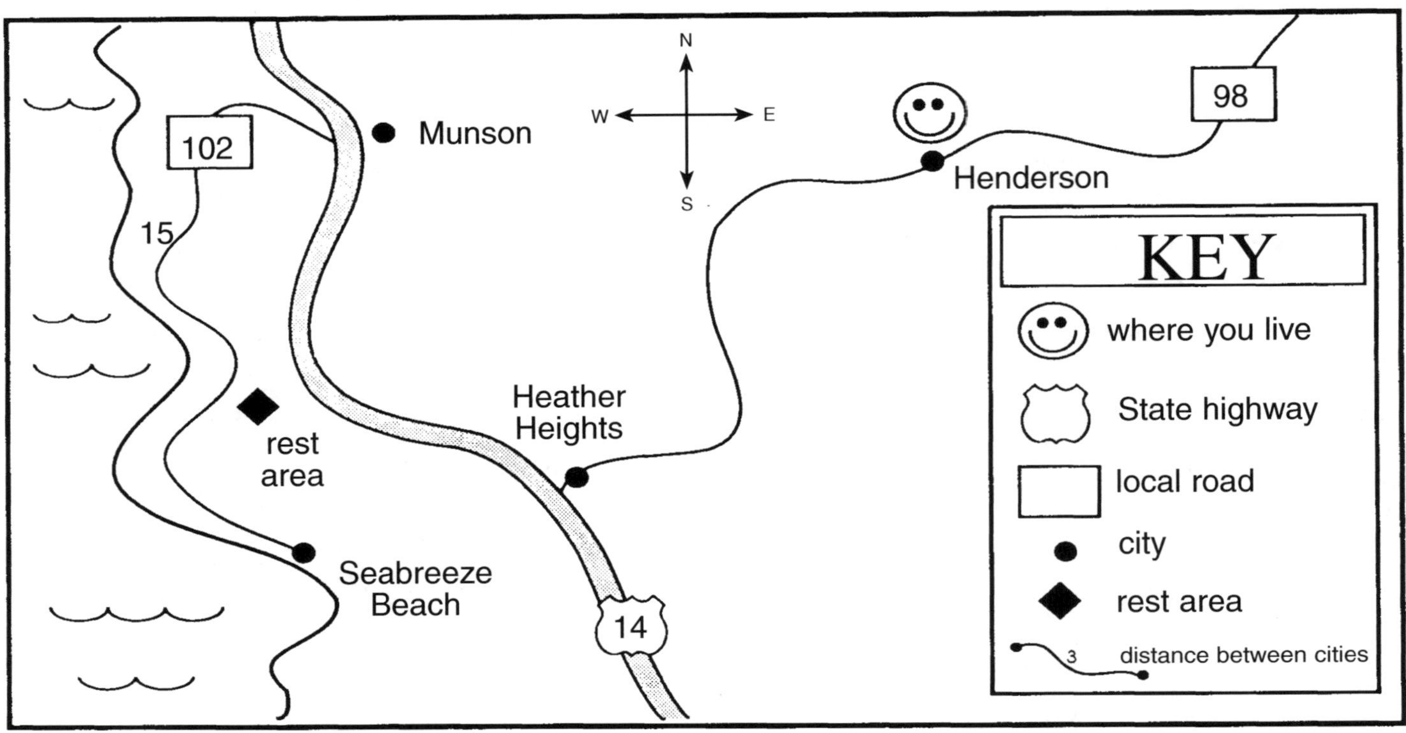

1. What road do we take to get out of Henderson? _______________________________

2. Do we travel west or east on 98? _______________________________

3. How many miles is it from Henderson to Heather Heights? _______________________

4. Once we get to Heather Heights, what road do we take? _______________________

5. Do we travel north or south on the highway? _______________________________

6. How many miles is it from Heather Heights to Munson? _______________________

7. What road do we take from Munson to Seabreeze Beach? _______________________

8. How many miles is it from Munson to Seabreeze Beach? _______________________

9. Is there a place to use the restroom before we get to the beach? _______________

10. How many miles is it from Henderson to Seabreeze Beach?_______________________

Product Maps

Sometimes maps can show us the types of things that are grown, raised, or mined in a certain place. We can see where the corn and cattle are grown and raised in Iowa. We can find out where the most wheat is grown in Saskatchewan. We can point to the places where apples are grown in Washington. We can see the spots where coal is mined in Pennsylvania. The types of maps that show us the types of things that are grown, raised, or mined are called product maps.

Look at this map that shows only some of the products grown, raised, or mined in Texas.

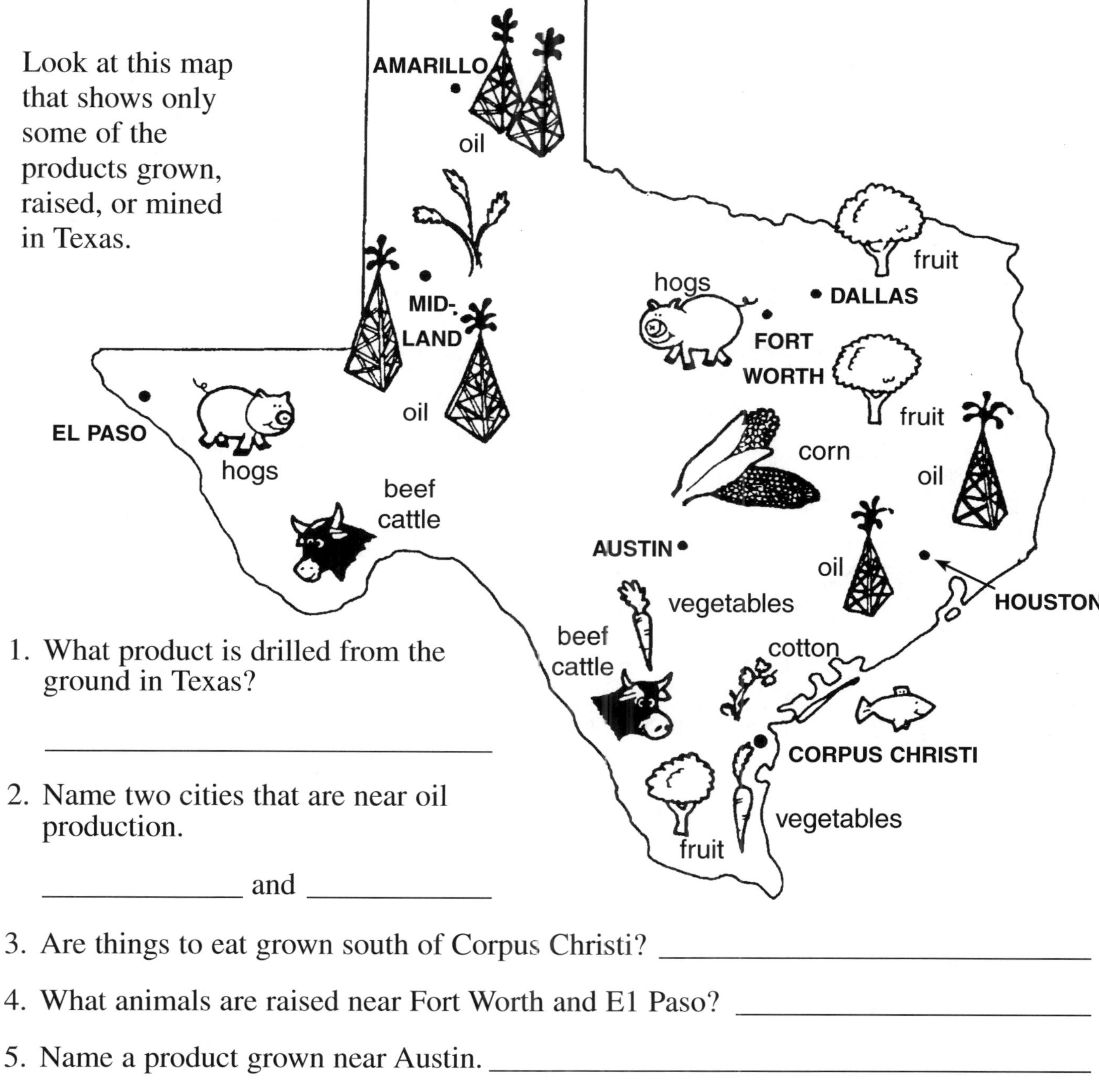

1. What product is drilled from the ground in Texas?

____

2. Name two cities that are near oil production.

_______________ and _____________

3. Are things to eat grown south of Corpus Christi? ________________________________

4. What animals are raised near Fort Worth and E1 Paso? ___________________________

5. Name a product grown near Austin. ____

Use an encyclopedia to find a product map for a place you are interested in. Share the map you find with your class.

In Producta...

This is the imaginary country of Producta. Read the map to find answers to the questions below.

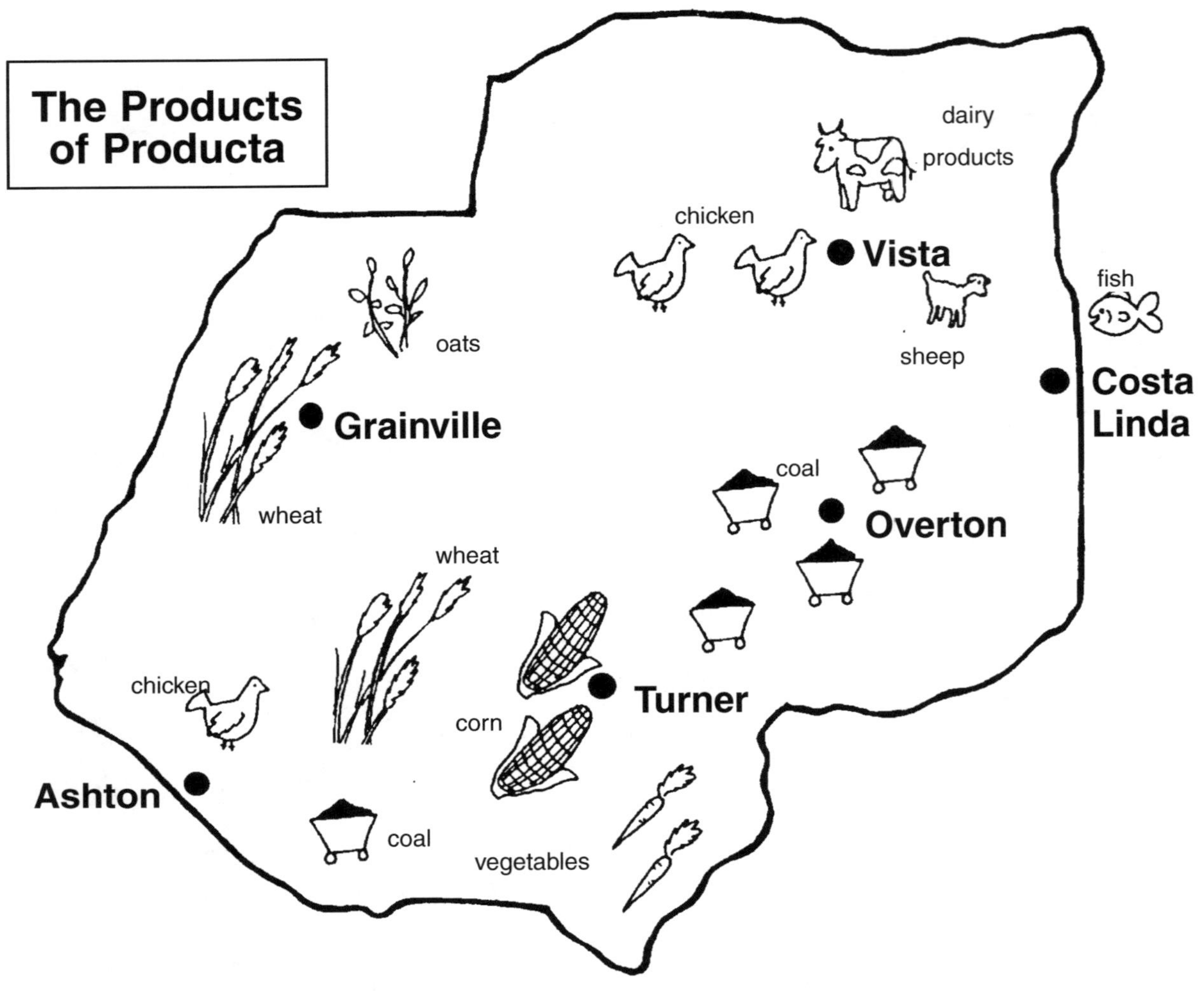

What products are grown or produced near these cities?

1. Overton? ____

2. Turner? ____

3. Costa Linda? ____

4. Grainville? ____

5. Vista? ____

Near what city are chicken, wheat, and coal produced? ____________________

In what city of Producta would you most like to live? ______________________

Why?____

Weather Maps

A map can show what the weather of a certain place has been or could be. There are a few different ways to make a weather map.

A weather map can use symbols to show the weather.

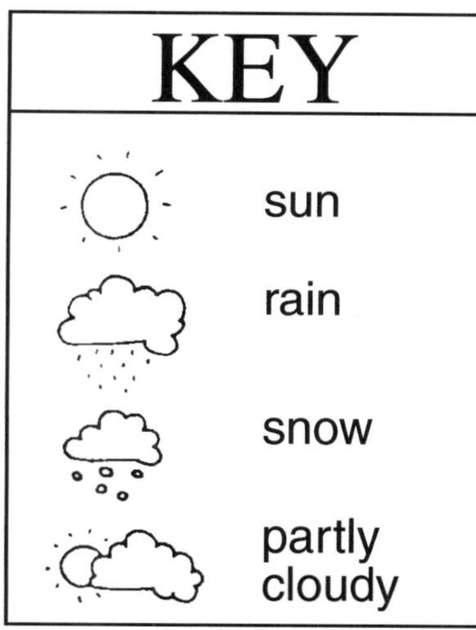

On the map above and the map below, color the area of rain blue, the area of sun yellow, the area of partly cloudy gray, and leave the area of snow uncolored.

A weather map can use kinds of shading to show the weather.

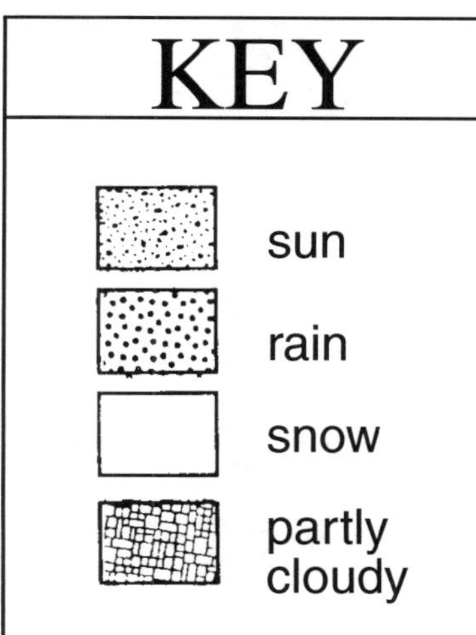

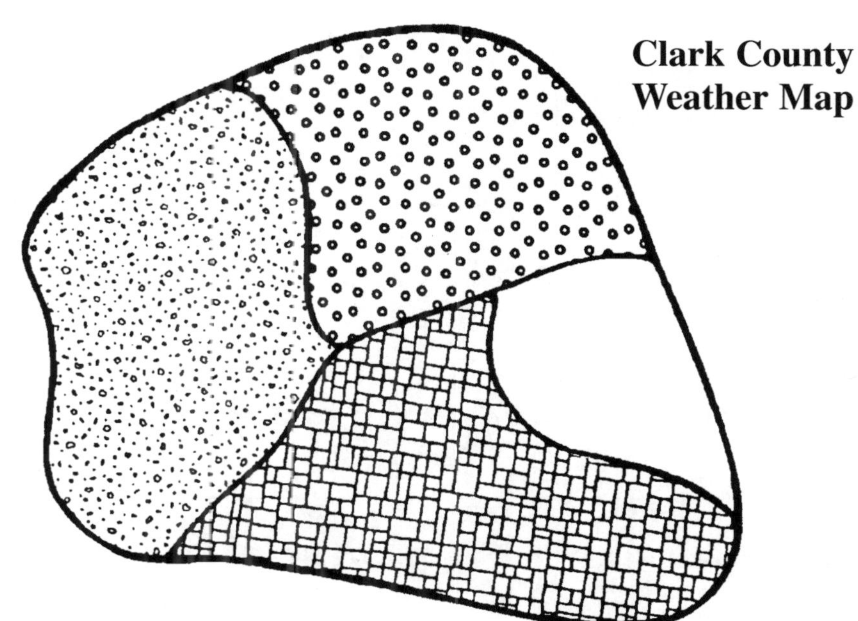

Use an encyclopedia or a newspaper to find a weather map. Share your map with the class.

Where Will It Rain?

Look at the weather map on this page. Use the map to answer the questions about the weather in certain states.

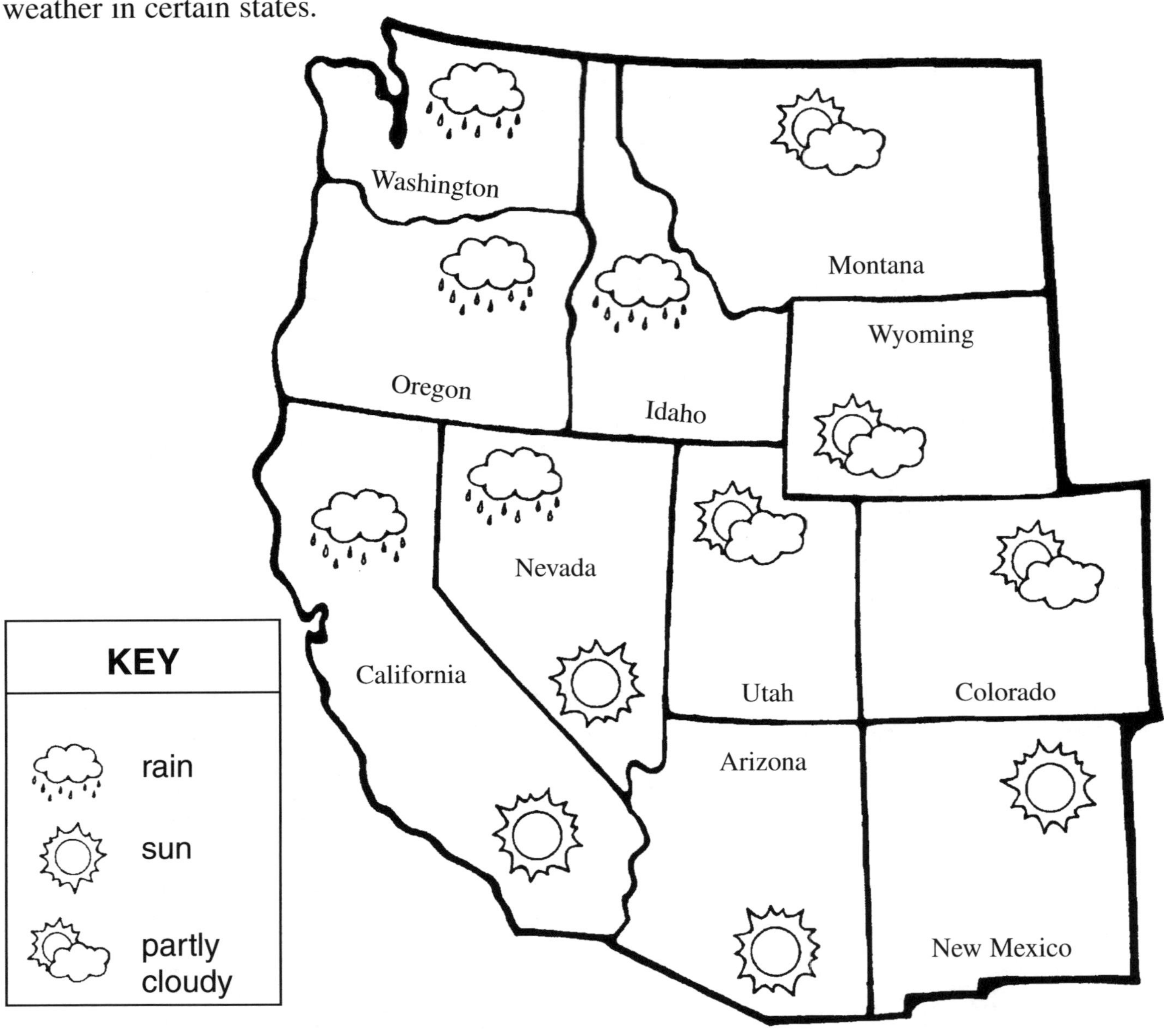

1. What states will only have rain? ________________ , ____________ and

   ____

2. In what states will the weather be partly cloudy? ________________ ,

   ________________ , ________________ and ________________

3. In what states will the northern part be rainy and the southern part be

   sunny? ________________ and ________________

4. What states will only have sun? ________________ and ____________

Beneath City Streets

What do you think is below the streets of a busy city? Are there gas and water pipes? Are there telephone and cable T.V. lines? Is there a sewer system?

> *Draw a map of what you think it looks like under a busy city street. Use a color key to show what is underground. Begin your map at a manhole cover.*

Warning: Do not go down under the streets on your own. It is dangerous!

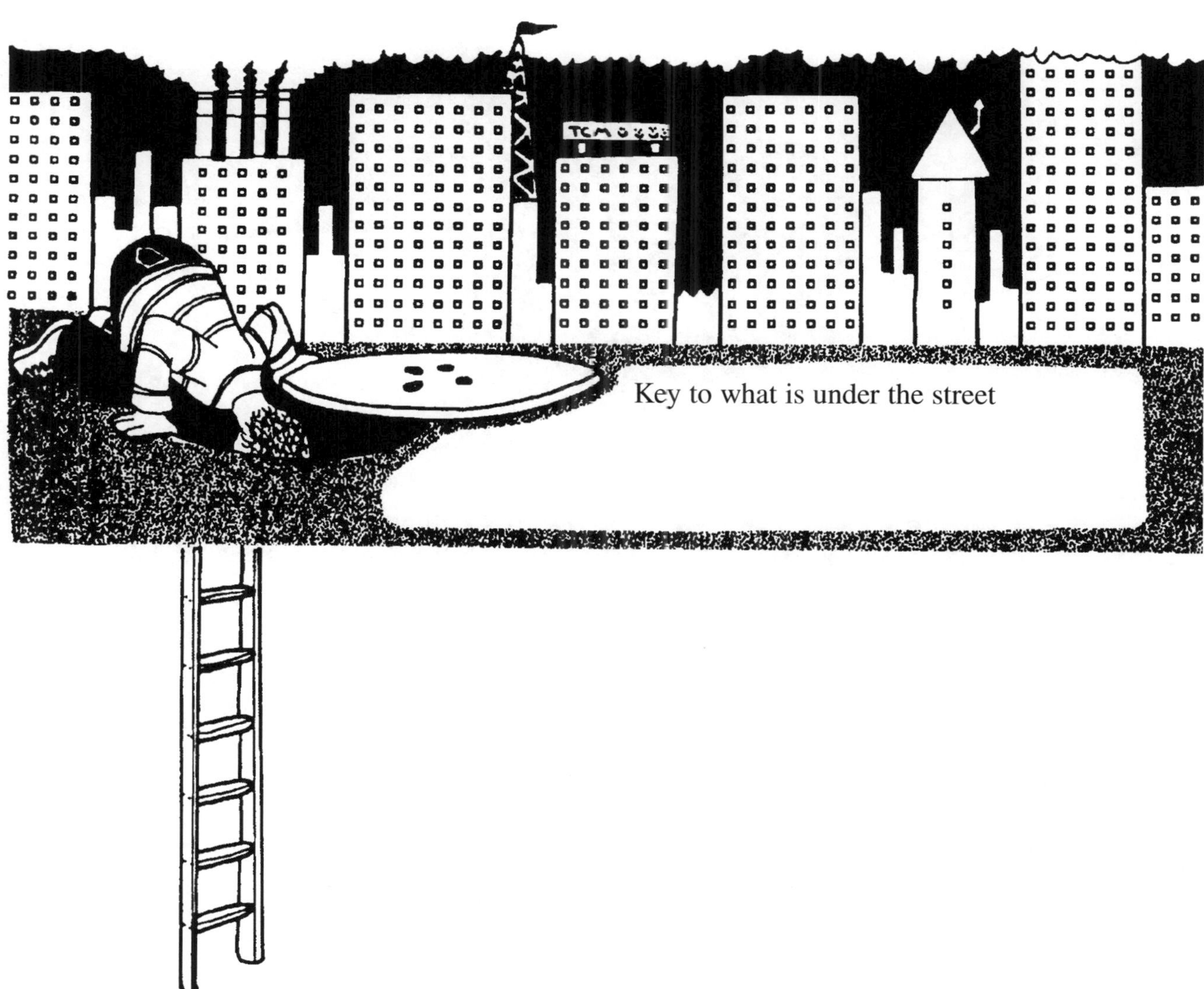

Invite someone from a city planning department to show you maps of what is below the streets of a busy city.

Population Map

A *population map* is a map that shows how many people live in a certain area. Usually, on a population map, a symbol of a person stands for a certain number of people.

If  stands for 100 people, how many people are there in the boxes below?

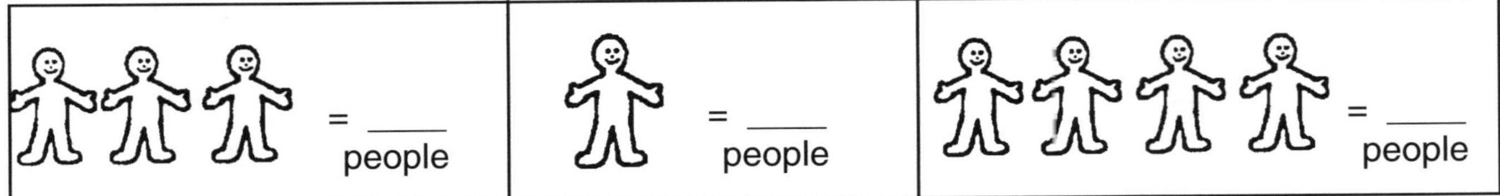

= _____ people

= _____ people

= _____ people

Read this map. How many people live in each of the areas of this imaginary country?

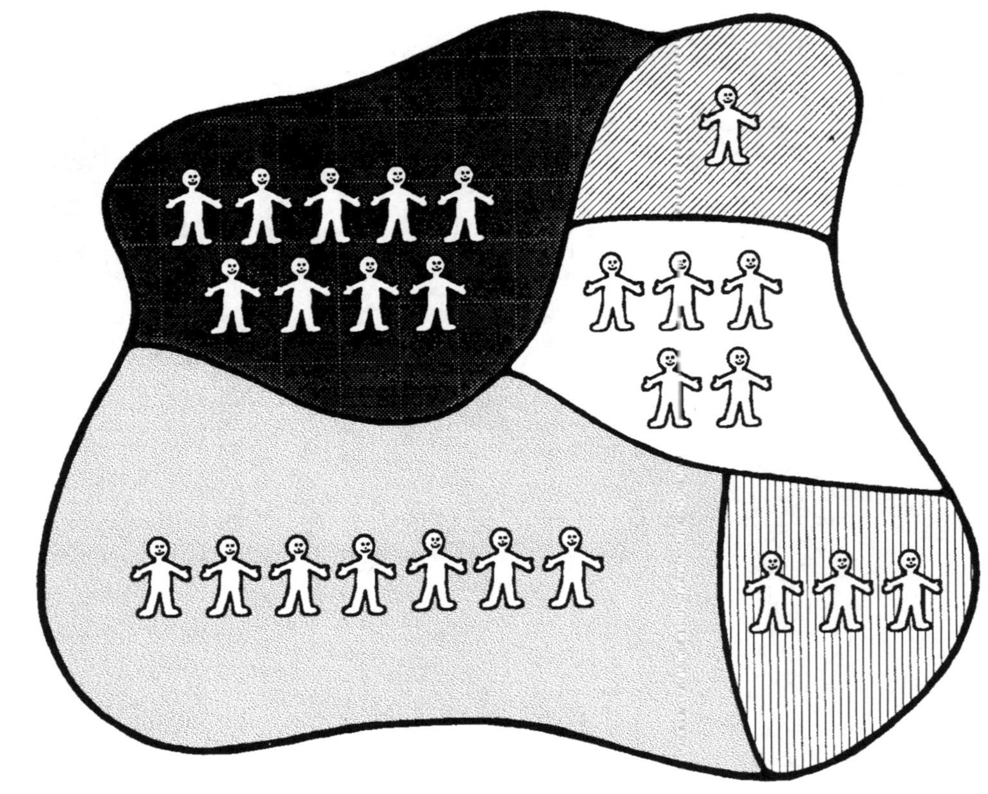

1. area = _____ people

2. area = _____ people

3. area = _____ people

4. area = _____ people

5. area = _____ people

Use an encyclopedia to find population maps. Share them with the class.

Treasure Map

Would you like to find a treasure map? If you did find a treasure map, you would have to follow the directions very clearly to find the treasure!

Write step-by-step directions that will tell where the treasure on this map is buried.

1. ____

2. ____

3. ____

4. ____

5. Dig at ✲ for buried treasure, just before the bushes.

You will need a partner for this next activity. Hide a "treasure" and create a map of where the treasure can be found. Give your map to your partner and see if he or she can read the map to find your treasure. Then, change places and let your partner hide a treasure for you to find.

From Words to Pictures

Make a map from the words on this page. Don't forget to fill in the key to your map. After you have made your map, reread the words. Does your map match the words exactly?

1. There are mountains in the north.

2. A lake is in the southeast corner.

3. A river runs from the mountains to the lake.

4. There is a thick forest on the west side of the river.

5. There is a town on the east side of the river, about halfway between the mountains and the lake.

KEY

mountains

lake

river

town

From Pictures to Words

Describe the location of as many things on this map as you can. For example, you may write, "The park is north of Green Street." After you have finished writing, read your words as you look at the map. Do your words make sense?

Ideas, Ideas, Ideas to Map!

On this page is a potpourri of map ideas for you to use with your students.

Manipulative Maps to Make

* Using blocks, linking shapes, or other building toys, encourage your students to construct a neighborhood. Each building toy will represent something "mapable" in the neighborhood.

* Using sand in a sandbox, twigs, leaves, and model toys, encourage your students to construct a sand city or countryside.

* Using paper, scissors, and glue, encourage students to draw, cut, and paste their school and playground on a large map made of construction or butcher paper.

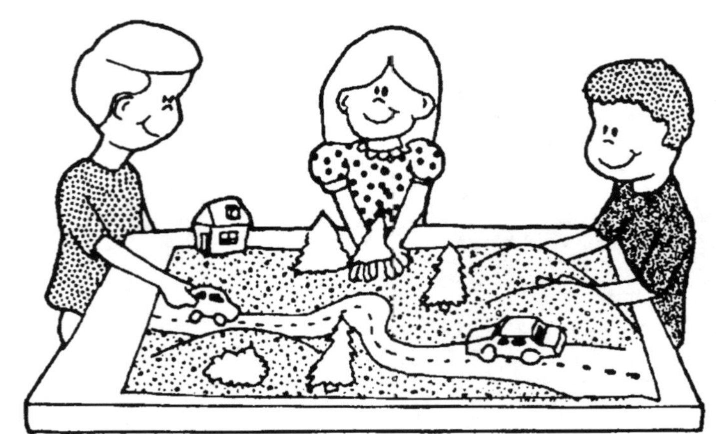

Many More Maps

The following maps can be created by your students as independent study activities, group projects, or class activities. Remind your students to include titles, labels, keys, scales, and directions on their maps.

- a make-believe place
- an underground city
- a hidden treasure
- a favorite place to go alone
- an exciting amusement park
- a zoo
- your neighborhood

- a future (or past) world
- your city
- your school
- your classroom
- your bedroom
- your house
- your state, country, or province

- to your best friend's house
- a park
- a road map
- a street
- another galaxy
- your dream house
- your choice!

Grid Page

Use this grid page for mapmaking activities.

Answer Key

p. 4

1. world
2. city
3. solar system
4. pretend world

p. 5

Check for accurate drawing.

p. 6

Answers will vary. Some ideas might be paper bags, sand, t-shirts, cookies, finger painting, etc.

p. 9

All should read: north-top; south-bottom; east-right; west-left.

p. 10

Ending square is bottom left corner square.

p. 11

1. north, south, east, west
2. north-south; east-west
3. north, south, west, east
4.

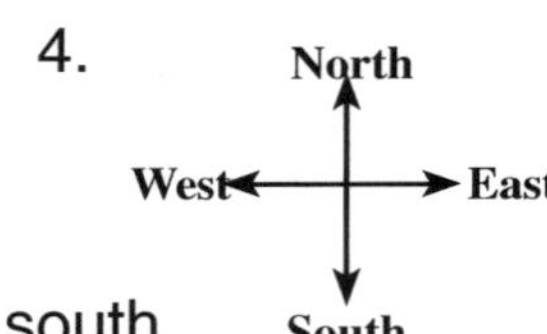

5. north, south
6. east, west
7. north, south
8. west, east

p. 12

Take 3 steps south.
Take 4 steps east.
Take 2 steps north.
Take 2 steps west.
Take 1 step north.
Take 4 steps east.
Take 4 steps south.
Take 6 steps west.

Take 3 steps south.
Take 3 steps east.

p. 14

1. sunrise
2. sunset
3. west
4. south, east

p. 16

The North Star is in the middle of the page, about a fourth down from the top. The pointer stars of the Big Dipper are in the middle of the page, about half way down.

p. 17

Words that should be crossed out are:

westsouth, eastnorth, westnorth, eastsouth

p. 18

1. north
2. north and south
3. southwest
4. 8
5. southeast
6. northeast
7. northeast and southeast

p. 19 & 20

Be sure the students build their compass roses with the north and south points the longest, the east and west points second longest, and the other points the smallest.

p. 21

Answers will vary. Ask students to tell you about their rooms. If you need to, ask a parent to check for accuracy.

p. 23

The camper needs to find the northeast campsite.

p. 24

1. Stop!
2. No bicycles
3. spring
4. Be quiet!
5. fire
6. sunshine

p. 26

1. 2
2. 5
3. forest
4. mountains
5. river

p. 28

1. school
2. south
3. Center
4. 5
5. Oak, Center, Elm, and First

p. 31

1. 1 mile
2. 2 inches, 2 miles
3. 6 inches, 6 miles
4. 2 miles
5. 4 inches, 4 miles

p. 32

1. 1 mile
2. 2 miles
3. 3 inches, 3 miles
4. 3 miles
5. 2 miles
6. 2 miles
7. 2 miles
8. 1 mile
9. 1 mile

Answer Key *(cont)*

p. 33
1. 2
2. 4
3. 1
4. 5
5. 3

p. 34
1. 2 miles
2. 5 kilometers

p. 35
1. 2 miles, 5 kilometers
2. 6 miles, 15 kilometers
3. 4 miles, 10 kilometers

p. 36
city park - 20 miles
your grandparents' house - 5 miles
zoo - 10 miles
movie theater - 15 miles
the ocean - 25 miles

p. 37
1. 900
2. 200
3. 500
4. 1,400
5. 800
6. 500
7. 1,500
8. 700

p. 38
1. northeast, 10
2. Taylor
3. 20
4. 10
5. 40, Cedarwood, 30
6. 60
7. 70
8. 130

p. 39
1. 11 meters
2. 6 meters
3. 12 meters
4. 8 meters
5. 17 meters

p. 40
1. My Bedroom
2. Rivertown
3. South America
4. Market Street

p. 41
1. Map C
2. Map B
3. Map A

p. 42
Check colors as a class activity.

p. 43
1. Texas
2. Virginia
3. Oklahoma
4. Idaho
5. Louisiana
6. Michigan

p. 45
1. Pluto
2. Jupiter
3. Jupiter, Saturn, Uranus, Neptune
4. Mercury
5. Venus, Mars

p. 46
Answers at top will vary.
Any order: North America, South America, Europe, Asia, Africa, Australia, Antarctica
Any order: Pacific Ocean, Atlantic Ocean, Arctic Ocean, Indian Ocean

p. 47
1. Atlantic Ocean (swim)
2. Asia (walk)
3. North America (walk)
4. Antarctica (walk)
5. Pacific Ocean (swim)
6. South America (walk)
7. Europe (walk)
8. Australia (walk)
9. Arctic Ocean (swim)
10. Africa (walk)

p. 48
1. Spin the globe or walk to the other side of it.
2. A globe, because it is round and it rotates.

p. 49
1., 2., and 3. Check colors
4. North America
5. South America
6. Antarctica

p. 50
3. North America, South America, Antarctica
4. Europe, Asia, Africa, Australia, Antarctica
5. Antarctica

p. 51
1. Southern, Eastern, and Western
2. Northern and Eastern
3. Eastern, Northern, and Southern
4. Southern and Eastern
5. Northern and Western

p. 57
from left to right
1. British Columbia
2. Alberta
3. Ontario
4. Quebec

Answer Key *(cont)*

p. 61

sun

1. bicycle
2. bed
3. boots
4. tree
5. bat and ball
6. B1
7. C3
8. A2

p. 62

1. A3
2. B1
3. B2
4. C3
5. A1 and A2
6. C2
7. B3
8. C1

p. 63

1. A1
2. C2
3. A4
4. B2
5. A2, A3
6. D2, D3, D4
7. B4
8. C1
9. D1
10. B1

p. 64

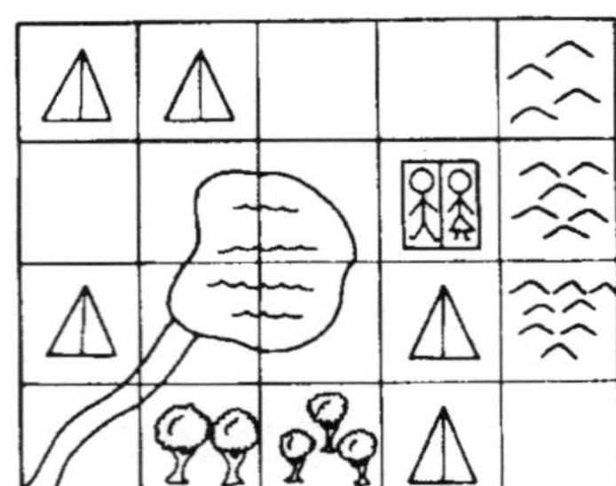

p. 65

1. Smithers, Bloomington, Charter
2. 243
3. 25, 30, 57
4. Smithers

p. 66

1. 98
2. west
3. 12 miles
4. 14
5. north
6. 8 miles
7. 102
8. 15 miles
9. yes
10. 35 miles

p. 67

1. oil
2. Midland, Houston, and/or Amarillo
3. yes
4. hogs
5. vegetables (or corn specifically)

p. 68

1. coal
2. vegetables, corn
3. fish
4. wheat, oats
5. animals; dairy cows, chicken, and sheep

Ashton

Answers will vary. Ask students to share their ideas with the class.

p. 70

1. Washington, Oregon, Idaho
2. Montana, Wyoming, Utah, Colorado
3. California, Nevada
4. Arizona, New Mexico

p. 72

Box 1 = 300

Box 2 = 100

Box 3 = 400

1. 900
2. 700
3. 300
4. 500
5. 100

p. 73

Answers will vary; this is a sample.

1. Get out of the boat and go 3 steps north.
2. Turn and travel 5 steps west past the rocks. Stop at the palm tree.
3. Go 2 steps southwest.
4. Take one step east.